THE BRING IT ON BOOK

SCREENPLAY / HOW-TO
+ NEVER-BEFORE-SEEN SCENES
TOGETHER FOREVER
FOR THE VERY FIRST TIME

FROM THE MOTHER OF *BRING IT ON*
JESSICA BENDINGER

THE BRING IT ON BOOK by Jessica Bendinger

Published by VERVE BALL, INC.

www.jessicabendinger.com

© 2020 Verve Ball, Inc.

Cover by Shauna Driscoll

ISBN: 9781887229586

TABLE OF CONTENTS

AUTHOR'S FOREWORD

BRING IT ON has become a cultural juggernaut.

It is a byproduct of teamwork and collaboration between myself, the director, the cast and the crew.

It is a movie about enthusiasm.

But it is also a movie about love.

It is because of that love that I worked from the fall of 1996-1999 and again in 2000, when director Peyton Reed asked me to write for the additional photography.

It is because of that love that I spent three years as part of a historic injunction on behalf of BRING IT ON and the 20,000 members of the WRITER'S GUILD OF AMERICA.

If you're doing your math, you'll know that it is because of that love that I worked on and fought for BRING IT ON for the better part of six years.

It all came from love.

Those who do not understand your love may call you difficult. They may call you challenging.

Not because they want you to love a little less.

They just want you to be quiet about your love.

They don't understand.

You've written a love letter to love.

And you're willing to fight for it.

When you write a love letter to love, a love letter to fairness, a love letter to what's true, people will have their relationship to it. And that's wonderful.

Success has many parents. This goes with the territory. When people have done questionable things, inappropriate or unkind things - things they would never do to a man - I cried.

But I didn't give up.

I was willing to parent this little outlier that could the best way I knew how. Imperfectly. Emphatically.

If it meant yelling, clapping, stomping and jumping up and down. I did it. I did what I had to do.

If they are being accurate and fair, they will say:

"She birthed it."

"She nursed it."

"She raised it."

People held the baby and burped the baby.

People changed the diaper.

I wasn't always liked.

I wasn't always compensated.

I wasn't always remunerated for the years of sacrifice.

There have been no apologies for the insults or slights incurred because of this child.

I love her for all she is and all she isn't.

Thank you for loving her.

JESSICA BENDINGER
The Mother of Bring It On

PART ONE:
THE PLAY BOOK

"I use a technique when I'm outlining – and I always outline – that is based on Jessica Bendinger, who wrote BRING IT ON. She did a guest post on John August's website – I don't know if I was in film school or just out of it at the time I read it – and she has the simple approach to generating story outline. It was three beats: the beginning, the middle and the end. And then you craft the beginning, middle and end... of the beginning, middle and end and so on. You build a story from all these mini-stories within the stories. I always do that no matter what project I'm working on."

BARRY JENKINS
DIRECTOR OF *MOONLIGHT* (2016),
ACADEMY AWARD FOR BEST PICTURE,
ACADEMY AWARD FOR BEST-ADAPTED SCREENPLAY
WRITTEN BY MAGAZINE

PART ONE: THE PLAYBOOK

INTRODUCTION

**How To Read (Or Write)
A Screenplay**

1)I AM A SCREENWRITER
CREATING ORIGINAL IDEAS
FOR FILM/TELEVISION (+ BEYOND)

2) SCREENPLAYS + SCRIPTS
ARE RECIPES FOR MAKING OTHER THINGS
(MOVIES, TV SERIES, EVEN 'REALITY' SHOWS - GASP!)

3) IF YOU ARE NEW
TO READING OR WRITING SCREENPLAYS, WELCOME!
PLEASE ENJOY THIS BRIEF TUTORIAL

INT. SCENE HEADING - DAY

Scene Headings like the one above are generally all caps and
explain location and time of day. INT. is short for interior
and EXT. means exterior. The hyphen - followed by DAY, NIGHT
or LATER adds timing/timelines to the mix.

INT. ACTION + DIALOGUE SECTION - MOMENTS LATER

This is action description. It's giving the reader a sense of
what's happening in the scene. Usually, it's about showing
not telling. I'm breaking that rule now.

We try not to have big BLOCKS of action description. A good
rule of thumb is THREE LINES. I'm breaking that rule now. For
you. JESS (that's me) is typing.

                    JESS
          When characters are introduced, we
          use caps like above. When we speak,
          it'll happen here. Under their
          name. Welcome to character and
          dialogue.
               (beat)
          More commonly known as 'people
          talking.'
          That parentheses above is what's
          called a parens. It can include
          instruction...
               (frowning)
          -- sharing a physical expression --
               (yelling)
          -- an obnoxious tone --
               (MORE)

JESS (CONT'D)
(taken aback)

-- or a visible reaction. 'Taken
aback,' is, um, kinda dumb. I laugh
when I see it and try not to use
it. But I hate rules, so --
(picking nose)
-- I'm breaking the rule! Parens
can also be construed as directing
the actor who will be speaking the
line, and some uptight scolds
really dislike it. I really dislike
uptight scolds!
(raspberry)
In the immortal words of Digital
Underground: 'Do what you like!'
That being said, the words below
these tell you <u>where to look.</u>

CLOSE ON: JESS'S PHONE

A TEXT reads: ***CLOSE ON, WIDER OR ANGLE ON TELL YOU WHERE <u>AND</u> WHAT TO LOOK AT. AND HOW WIDE OR HOW CLOSE. ENTIRELY OPTIONAL. ECU - for example - MEANS EXTREME CLOSE UP.***

NEW TEXT: ***I TRY TO USE THESE WITH DISCRETION BUT I AM FREQUENTLY INDISCREET.***

NEW TEXT NOTIFICATION DINGS: ***BTW important 'SOUNDS' also get ALL CAPS. Introducing CHARACTERS onscreen for the first time get CAPS. I like my imaginary onscreen text italicized and in bold. Many argue on this. I say: ladies choice! Writer's choice!***

Another TEXT: ***I'VE WRITTEN SOME OF THIS BOOK IN SCREENPLAY FORMAT. OTHER PARTS ARE IN REGULAR OLD WORDS.***

WIDER REVEALS JESS, standing in an echo-chamber.

JESS (CONT'D)
Did you enjoy the screenplay
formatting tutorial coming to you
via text? Cheeky, I know.
(sneezing)
I put a sneeze in a parens to break
up this note about transitions like
CUT TO, MATCH CUT TO, etcetera. I
will do a match cut now. Hang on --

Jess SNEEZING quasi-violently as --

MATCH CUT TO:

INT. KITCHEN - NEXT DAY

-- MINNIE the chihuahua mix SNEEZING. Jess pets her cute dog before grabbing a COFFEE CUP.

>   JESS
>   You'll see the word 'continuous'
>   which is doing lots of work. I'm
>   kidding. It's just telling you to
>   keep reading. It's not essential,
>   but it's around. It speaks to
>   continuity. It's a controlling way
>   of letting you know we're flowing
>   between bits even if there's no
>   transition.

Minnie BARKS. Then begins SPEAKING. In a heavy Liverpudlian accent, epitomizing canine magnificence.

>   MINNIE
>   Sorry to interrupt, but some
>   screenwriters hate transitions and
>   rarely use them. As a dog - who
>   lives life low to the ground - I
>   will say I feel an odd camaraderie
>   with transitions
>   'cause they're at the bottom of a
>   scene.

>   JESS
>   Very insightful, Minnie. As I was
>   saying, 'continuous' will soon be
>   telling the production team they
>   need a coffee cup, whilst
>   suggesting to the cinematographer
>   and editor...how they might make or
>   break this next piece of shtick.

INT. COFFEE CUP - CONTINUOUS

ANGLE ON: TINY-SIZED JESS inside Big Jess's COFFEE CUP holding a TEENY MEGAPHONE. Her mouth is moving, but we can't hear her.

>   JESS
>   We can't hear you.

>   TINY JESS
>   (into teeny megaphone)
>   I'm not shtick! I'm an integral
>   part of the story. By the way --
>   (sotto)
>   (MORE)

                   TINY JESS (CONT'D)
     -- 'sotto' is another overused
     parens, but since we adore using
     orchestral terms whenever possible,
     we have to include it.

CLOSE ON: Tiny Jess getting comfy at the bottom of the cup,
lowering the megaphone and speaking directly to camera.

                   TINY JESS (CONT'D)
     Facing the camera and talking is
     called 'breaking the third wall'
     and means the character is talking
     directly to the audience. That
     means you, buster.
     As you've surmised, (CONT'D) means
     this character keeps on going
     regardless of whether you want them
     to keep talking or not. Don't be
     intimidated.
         (whispering)
     Screenwriting software does this
     automatically. Unless it is hung-
     over.
         (into megaphone)
     In all sincerity, I feel that
     whispering into a teeny megaphone
     while inside a coffee cup is
     nothing short of enchanting. I've
     learned to indulge these things.
     Oh, look --

A GIANT COFFEE POT looming over the cup o' Tiny Jess, about
to pour.

                   TINY JESS (CONT'D)
     -- don't freak out. This is all
     make believe. That's quite steamy
     but it's gonna be okay. I'm just
     swimming in Lake Me! I am in the
     kitchen and I can stand the heat --

INT. KITCHEN - DAY

Jess pouring a fresh dose of black gold into the cup.

                   TINY JESS (O.S.)
     -- aaaaahhhhhhhh! That's super
     frickin hot! You forgot to tell
     them O.S. means off screen. And
     V.O. is voice-over! And hot is hot!

Big Jess blows on the drink, slurping and sighing.

                    JESS
          In that spirit, please enjoy this
          tutorial. Dedicated to Lake You.

The ROOM TILTS as everything slides off screen, replaced by
an amazing DANCE CREW carrying a SIGN that reads: WHY I
WRITE.

CHAPTER ONE

Why I Write

INT. JESS'S HOUSE - EVENING

Jess sits at her laptop in dark silhouette, wondering OUT
LOUD how to do this book.

>   JESS
> I write to try and understand
> things and share them. I write to
> teach myself and to heal myself and
> explore big problems. Disguising
> those quests as entertainment.
>   (shrugging)
> Now that we got that out of the
> way, I suppose you wanna know
> what's gonna be in this thing,
> right? That's so weird! So do I!
> Jinx!

A FLASHLIGHT pierces the darkness, illuminating a FINGER
shushing.

>   JESS (CONT'D)
> I thought it would be cute if two
> things happen here. I can't believe
> no one has done this yet, so keep
> it to yourself.

SCREENPLAYS illuminated by SEARCHLIGHTS begin falling around
her, Jess dodging unsuccessfully.

>   JESS (CONT'D)
> As you may have noticed, I thought
> it would be cool to write this
> guide in my preferred format: the
> screenplay. I have never seen it
> done this way and - well - since
> *it's what I do*, I think it might be
> fun. Catchy. Weird. Addictive.
> Kinda like BRING IT ON. Heads up:
> time travel in 3, 2 --

INT. 1980'S - WHITE SOUNDSTAGE - FLASHBACK

TEEN JESS' wearing a Madonna-inspired outfit, dancing like
she's in the famous *"Lucky Star"* video.

                    TEEN JESS
     -- remember when new characters
     appear on the page, their arrival
     gets all caps? Look alive, my
     friend -- here comes the Madonna *Of
     My Mind*.

MADONNA suddenly switch-kicks into frame.

                    MADONNA
     "You must be my lucky star..."

                    JESS
     When I first wanted to try
     screenwriting way back in the 80s,
     there were only, like, three books
     anyone had heard of. Right, Madge?

                    MADONNA
     There was 'ADVENTURES IN THE SCREEN
     TRADE,' by William "Bo" Goldman
     which has a screenplay in it. For
     BUTCH CASSIDY and THE SUNDANCE KID.

                    JESS
     But it isn't really <u>about</u>
     screenwriting.

                    MADONNA
     What about Syd Field's book,
     SCREENPLAY?

                    JESS
     Madge. Someone also recommended
     THE ART OF DRAMATIC WRITING, by
     Lajos Negri. I wanted to love it
     cause the author's name was so
     fantastic but none of it really
     spoke to me. Not like you do.

                    MADONNA
     Are you gonna tell them why you'll
     be invoking a stellar cast of
     imaginary celebrity friends?

                    JESS
     Are you suggesting we're not real
     friends? To my face? That's just
     bizarre.
          (to camera)
     I invent imaginary friends because
     I was a lonely child. Imaginary
     friends were my safe place. Thus,
     screenwriting.
                    (MORE)

                      JESS (CONT'D)
You can create as big a posse as
your heart desires! On the page.

A SINGLE TEAR rolls down Madonna's cheek, streaking her
mascara.

                      JESS (CONT'D)
Are you crying?

                      MADONNA
Allergies.
    (then)
If you're wondering why there's no
CUT TO or transition below -
sometimes writers leave it out. As
the queen of reinvention, I am big
on mood-slash-preference kinda
things. Like me.

EXT. UCLA - 1980'S

80s JESS stomps around UCLA wearing Doc Martens and ripped
jeans. "DON'T YOU FORGET ABOUT ME," playing softly in the
background as Jess speaks in VOICEOVER aka V.O.

                      JESS (V.O.)
Eventually, I even took a
screenwriting course at UCLA. And
none of it resonated. There were
all these terms and rules about act
breaks and midpoints and, inciting
incidents and well -- things that
didn't speak to me.
    (speaking to camera)
So. I called hooey on that. There
is no one way to do anything,
people. Sorry. I mean, they did a
study about doing dishes. There are
lotsa ways to do dishes. Hundreds.
    (tugging at her shirt)
Lotsa kinds of shirts. No single
way to make shirts. Hundreds of
ways. So people who say there's
only one way are usually selling
you something. Like me, now. With
this book.

Pulling open a door --

INT. LECTURE HALL - CONTINUOUS

-- heading into a 1980's SCREENWRITNG LECTURE in progress.

                    JESS
               (disrupting class)
          It's an idea! We're making recipes
          for other things. Let's make peace
          with that. Don't overcomplicate it.
          Unless overcomplication is your
          thing.

                    PROFESSOR
          Please sit down. Unless you'd like
          to teach the class.

                    JESS
          Oh, I will be teaching this class,
          mister. To a group of eight
          graduate students. In thirty years,
          my friend.

                    CLASS
          Shut up!/Sit down!/Love your
          outfit!/Don't forget to tell them
          when many people talk at once you
          can group it together under one
          heading!

                                        CUT TO:

INT. BARNES + NOBLE - EARLY 90S

Jess reading a stack of books in AISLE 3.

                    JESS
          Those students were kinda harsh,
          right? So, like any financially-
          strapped, aspiring young writer, I
          started reading whatever spoke to
          me. For free. In a bookstore.
          Remember those? I was trying to
          figure screenwriting out.

QUICK CUTS of: *THE ARTIST'S WAY; CREATIVE VISUALIZATION;*
WISHCRAFT; WRITE IT DOWN, MAKE IT HAPPEN.

                    JESS (CONT'D)
          And what I figured out was this:
          screen-writing books? Didn't
          interest me. And self-help and
          personal growth books were much
          more inspiring. Much easier to
          understand.
               (to the heavens)
          I needed inspiration!
               (beat)
                    (MORE)

                        JESS (CONT'D)
          Besides, I'd heard Hollywood was a
          brutal dumpster fire of betrayal
          and bad behavior, so self-help
          books helped me cope for this in
          advance. Pre-hearsal, if you will.

P.A. SYSTEM crackling with STATIC.

                        BOOKSTORE EMPLOYEE (O.S.)
          To the customer sitting in Aisle 3,
          don't forget to tell them about
          'VARIOUS' and 'MONTAGE' and that
          you can use action descriptions to
          scoot to different locations or
          settings efficiently. We're closing
          in five minutes. So, like, scoot.

INT. COMING-OF-AGE FLASHBACKS - VARIOUS

- YOUNG JESS is buried in a copy of Judy Blume's classic,
FOREVER.

                        YOUNG JESS
          I was always reading about things I
          was interested in or curious about -
          - which was -- um, you know --
                (biting lip, self-
                 conscious)
          -- sex and Hollywood. I learned
          about sex from Judy Blume.
                (whispering)
          Thanks, Judy.

WIDER REVEALS Judy Blume reading over Jess's shoulder,
winking. Suddenly --

- PRETEEN JESS springs out of Young Jess's body and begins
walking through a GIANT BOOK FOREST. BOOKS THE SIZE OF
BUILDINGS line her path.

                        PRETEEN JESS
          I learned about sex and Hollywood
          reading juicy bestsellers.
          Bestsellers that were --
                (winking)
          -- for mature audiences only?

SCRUPLES by Judith Krantz, HOLLYWOOD WIVES by Jackie Collins,
MASTER OF THE GAME by Sidney Sheldon.

                        PRETEEN JESS (CONT'D)
          It was an indirect route -- to be
          sure.
                (MORE)

>   PRETEEN JESS (CONT'D)
> But in the pre-internet eighties,
> books were the biggest thing
> around.

- COLLEGE JESS reading: ADVENTURES in THE SCREEN TRADE by
William Goldman, CRACKPOT by John Waters, INDECENT EXPOSURE
by David McClintick.

>   COLLEGE JESS
> But if Hollywood was as bad as
> fiction and non-fiction authors
> said it was, I was going to need
> some guidance. Stat. And until
> then, I'd take every writing job I
> could get.

CLOSE ON: SPIN MAGAZINE COVER.

>   COLLEGE JESS (CONT'D)
> Interning at SPIN Magazine led to
> my first writing jobs.

WIDER reveals COLLEGE JESS riding up an elevator nervously.

>   COLLEGE JESS (CONT'D)
> Interviewing hip hop icons Salt-n-
> Pepa.

- FLASHBACK: Icons SALT-N-PEPA speak very candidly to Jess at
the NEXT PLATEAU Records offices in New York in late 80's.

>   COLLEGE JESS (CONT'D)
> Understatement alert: this would
> have a profound impact and
> influence on me. Something these
> hip hop legends said hit me like a
> ton of bricks.

>   80'S SALT
> It's not about, 'Young women of
> America...listen.' That's not fun,
> messages in every rap song. I love
> Public Enemy and I love their
> messages...but everybody's not
> black.

>   80'S PEPA
> We want both audiences. We want to
> please the crowd.

>   COLLEGE JESS
> As someone who loved Salt-n-Pepa's
> music and Public Enemy's music,
> this caught my attention.

INT. SPIN MAGAZINE OFFICES - LATE 80S - DAY

Colllege Jess is trying to connect a GIANT CASSETTE RECORDER to a PHONE. It's not going well.

                    COLLEGE JESS
               (to camera)
          I was listening. To both artists. I
          loved Salt-n-Pepa. I loved Public
          Enemy. I loved them both. It wasn't
          an either/or. It was a both/and.

Jess presses RECORD and dials. Her editor, JOHN LELAND, pops his head in.

                    JOHN LELAND
          Are you gonna tell them what Chuck
          D says really sticks with you? For
          a long time?
               (off her nod)
          I mean, it's not overstating it to
          say, that this moment will take
          root in you and never really leave.

                    COLLEGE JESS
          You're not helping, here.

                    JOHN LELAND
               (to camera)
          I want you to imagine you are
          finishing college and stupidly
          excited to be talking to the artist
          you've been listening to nonstop.
          You are starstruck. You are
          intimidated. Your editor is
          standing over your shoulder in your
          mind.

                    COLLEGE JESS
          I can still hear you. I'm very
          nervous --

                    JOHN LELAND
          You really want to hear what this
          person has to say. It's important
          to you! You are in college,
          interviewing your favorite MC. You
          could lose this job at any moment.
          Good luck.

SPEAKER PHONE is RINGING, RINGING, RINGING.

                    COLLEGE JESS
          Like any inexperienced, clueless
          college student, I freeze. All I
          can get out is: "Why PUBLIC ENEMY?"

80'S CHUCK D talks into a telephone.

                    80'S CHUCK D
          It's to the public that totally
          believes in the goodness of the
          system and that believes that the
          system is good. I'm their enemy
          because the system is not good and
          the system has treated black people
          on the whole in one of the cruelest
          manners in [the history of]
          mankind. And this is the same
          system that...had blacks in slavery
          and bondage for three hundred years
          and then another mental slavery
          that's going on now...

College Jess STUNNED by how honest Chuck is being. She
mouths WOW. Behind her, the entire STAFF is listening,
looking at each other, like, WOW. Thumbs up.

                    JESS
          Holy crap. Poetry and honesty! What
          else would you expect from Chuck D?
          In case you were wondering what
          might've inspired me to write BRING
          IT ON. Those two interviews. Those
          artists speaking candidly. About
          messages. About audiences.

                                        MATCH CUT TO:

INT. DESERT FLATS - DAY

CLOSE ON: CAR STEREO playing PUBLIC ENEMY'S classic *YOU'RE
GONNA GET YOURS*. DUST flying.

                    JESS
          After BRING IT ON is the number one
          movie in the country for two weeks
          in a row, people kinda wanted to
          know how I got the idea. I think
          maybe now you know.

WIDER revealing Jess driving with the top down. TRAMP by SALT-
N-PEPA taking over the car's SPEAKERS.

                    JESS (CONT'D)
Very special thanks to Chuck-D,
Sandra 'Pepa' Denton and Cheryl
'Salt' James. Big inspiration.

Jess hits the brakes, creating serious drifting DUST.

                    JESS (CONT'D)
Now - sometimes people ask me for
my screenwriting techniques. Or to
read their script. Or loan them
money. Sometimes both.

Doing donuts, Jess is lowering dust GOGGLES.

                    JESS (CONT'D)
       (smiling)
In the early aughts, I wrote it
down. I wanted it to be simple.
Easy to understand. Relatable!
       (gesturing)
How I BROUGHT IT ON OUT, if you
will.
       (victory arms)
A BRING IT ON...OUT --
       (whispering)
-- out-lining, guide --
       (indoor voice)
-- process thingy, if you will. A
play-blog? Is that word taken?

SIRENS. COP CAR in pursuit.

                    COPS (O.S.)
Pull over. That's not a word.
You're under arrest --

                    JESS
It's a quick treatise on picking
the world of your story and
generating an outline. You might
even call it... Chapter Two: How I
Write.

Jess flooring it, racing past a billboard that reads: CHAPTER
TWO: HOW I WRITE.

CHAPTER TWO

HOW I WRITE

I think of myself as a very non-linear, intuitive writer. I have discipline and focus when I need it, but I allow myself to be very messy and unfocused and all-over-the-place, and I find both ends of the spectrum very useful (as you'll see from this response)! I find balance through exploring the two extremes, then using them in a conscious way. I can get very bored, so this vacillation serves me well.

My process has many parts to it. There's no simple answer. I'll say with as much authority as I can muster through text:

"BEWARE THE EASY, ONE-SIZE-FITS-ALL ANSWER!"

There are many ways to come up with ideas, write outlines and birth screenplays. The biggest journey we all have is finding out what works for us, and the beauty of that is that it will be so radically different for everyone. But as for me? I believe in following my enthusiasm, my curiosity and my fear. Not necessarily in that order.

THE WORLD

For stories, I begin by exploring arenas and worlds I am secretly or overtly enthusiastic about.

- What lights me up?
- What do I want to try, go, do, be, see?
- What are my closet fascinations?
- What are the things I secretly search or seek out at the bookstore or library?
- Who and what am I drawn to?

If it's a really personal or compulsive fascination that I wouldn't necessarily discuss with just anyone, or a theme that is so intrinsic to my fantasy life or dream life that it's almost invisible? Then I am really onto something. These are where my best ideas for arenas are born. This process of warming to an area can take me a while. My big ideas are gestating for a long time before I even get to story, character or outline. Sometimes I'll get random scene ideas or visuals, and I just tuck them away. I know they'll be useful eventually, or might lead me somewhere I'm supposed to go and were merely a conduit. The point is, this part can be meandering for me. When it starts really pulling my attention, or filling me with images and ideas I know it's time for arena to meet story.

THE STORY

Once I have the arena, then it's onto the story itself. If

I'm unclear, I use a question method to spitball ideas, or will start randomly combining things that interest me without attachment to outcome. For Bring It On, that was simple: I was bananas for those crazy cheerleading competitions, and I loved hip hop and started asking 'what if?' Hip hop's assimilation and appropriation into the culture had been so thorough, I thought, "How can I illustrate that in a fun way?" I started there and kept asking "what if" questions until I got a story that felt really fun, meaningful and juicy for me.

- What if the best squad in the country had been cheating?
- What if the squad they'd been stealing from was sick of it?
- What if the perp tried to make it right?

As I said earlier, I resist easy answers...so my remedy for that malaise is almost always questions. Questions are at the heart of my process, and I keep asking them until I have an idea I am happy with.

THE CHARACTER

Once I have arena and story, I like to hit the brakes and move into character in a pretty in-depth way. That means more questions.

- Who is the character?

- What is their core fear? Core desire? Core problem? What do they 'think' they want?

- What do they need to heal/thrive/evolve?

- What do they believe they need or think their goal is, versus the real need and real goal necessary for meaningful transformation in their life?

To recap: The story you're telling is about the problem you and your hero are solving. Storytelling is problem-solving. And it's a superpower.

This distance - between what they think they need and what they really need? That journey is your story.

The tension of that discrepancy helps me to build the narrative. But I'm of the "Character Is Plot" school, so this stuff is my fuel. Otherwise, the process is just too flat for me, and I get really bored. I want a thorough understanding of who he/she is emotionally, intellectually, physically and spiritually. I use those four markers to give my characters substance, and each marker is invaluable to me. If a character is an agnostic or an atheist, for example, that knowledge gives me a valuable place from which to understand how they operate in the world. If someone is a people-pleaser because they were neglected as a child, I can play with that. It serves me to understand what 'potential reactions' for that character might be given the confines of the idea...even if that is never announced anywhere in the script! I revel in knowing what the inner push-pulls are before I dive into story, so the world around the character can toss him where he needs to go.

THE OUTLINE

Once I have the character and the idea, I start working the story beats out from macro to micro in this outline process.

<u>ROUND ONE (aka Three Big Beats):</u>
1. The Beginning
2. The Middle
3. And End

<u>ROUND TWO (aka Nine Medium-Sized Beats):</u>
The beginning, middle and end of the (drumroll, please) beginning, middle and end! It can look like this:

1. The Beginning of the Beginning
2. The Middle of the Beginning
3. The End of the Beginning

4. The Beginning of the Middle
5. The Middle of the Middle
6. The End of the Middle

7. The Beginning of the End
8. The Middle of the End
9. The End of the End

<u>ROUND THREE (aka Twenty-Seven Bitty Beats):</u>
The beginnings, middles and ends of each of the aforementioned beginnings, middles and ends.

This looks pretty silly when spelled out, but I'm a super fan of silly, so here goes:

1. **The Beginning of the Beginning**
2. The Middle of the Beginning
3. The End of the Beginning
4. The Beginning of the Middle of the Beginning
5. The Middle of the Middle of the Beginning
6. The End of the Middle of the Beginning
7. The Beginning of the End of the Beginning
8. The Middle of the End of the Beginning
9. The End of the End of the Beginning **AKA End of Act One**

10. The Beginning of the Beginning of the Middle
11. The Middle of the Beginning of the Middle

12. The End of the Beginning of the Middle
13. The Beginning of the Middle of the Middle
14. **The Middle of the Middle**
15. The End of the Middle
16. The Beginning of the End of the Middle
17. The Middle of the End of the Middle
18. The End of the End of the Middle **AKA End of Act Two**

19. The Beginning of the Beginning of the End
20. The Middle of the Beginning of the End
21. The End of the Beginning of the End
22. The Beginning of the Middle of the End
23. The Middle of the Middle of the End
24. The End of the Middle of the End
25. The Beginning of the End of the End
26. The Middle of the End of the End
27. **The End of the End AKA End of Act Three**

EXPERIMENT

I used to use eleven beats per act and thirty-three total for my outlines, but I always ended up with scenes I didn't need. I've grown to prefer a really tight first pass because it's easier for me to see what's missing when I'm not floating in excess. But sometimes I over-write, and whittle down, too. It really depends on my mood. If I can beef up twenty-seven scenes into three or four pages per scene, I'm looking at a nice, first rough draft.

FIRST DRAFTS, or VOMIT DRAFTS

After I have my outline, I like to just spew these out. I'm not a precious writer. I'm constitutionally incapable of slaving over my first pass. That's second and third pass shtick for me unless I'm on a rewrite. My goal is simply to write without editing and write it as badly as possible. I want to write the crappiest piece of crap I can and claim that as my goal. Why? Because that goal shuts up the critic and let's me work. If I set out to suck, the critic can't bitch at me. We are in agreement!

In the end, the results are never as bad as I think they will be, and I have something to work with. And when things suck, this is quite useful: I have something concrete to push against for the next pass. Sucking is actually a critical part of my process, and I embrace it. There's nothing like reading something that doesn't work to get your wheels spinning about fixing it and making things better. I'm very permissive with the first pass: anything and everything goes…except not trying. Trying and failing is a big, big win for me. Not trying is not okay.

SECOND AND THIRD PASSES

After a second pass of refining and improving and really trying to tickle myself, it's time to share a draft with a trusted reader. This can be anyone whose opinion is meaningful to me. I want notes I can use, so I choose my readers wisely. I do another pass of notes and tweak once or twice, and then I let it go. If it's an assignment, it's never fully done and it seems like there are always changes (even if the movie is shooting). I try to be flexible and not get too attached.

REWRITES

My rewrite mindset is different from my original writing mindset, mind you. I can detach more easily on rewrites, but I have cultivated some grace and flexibility when getting notes. Nobody likes a defensive writer - particularly me - so I've made it my business to cultivate some resilience during the notes process. Being attached on some level means I don't believe I can generate more, or that things can only happen one way; and neither of those things is true. There is always more. There are always options and other ways of seeing things. Hopefully this serves me - and the material! - well.

A NORMAL DAY AT WORK

There is no such thing as a normal day at work! It's always different. I wake up, get my coffee and walk my dog for a good half hour. The morning walk clears my head and helps me go over what needs to get done. Picking up dog crap and caring for something besides yourself keeps you humble and grounded.

If I'm on a rewrite, I set goals and rewards for myself to help motivate me. Writing can be lonely, and there aren't always pats on the back, so it's up to me to build those in. I take lots of breaks and make it a priority to be good to myself: snacks, lots of water, a good stretch or a workout, quickie meditations or baths, hanging out with friends and walks. I need to meditate a few times a day or I get off-balance. Normal for me is mixing it up, I guess. I don't ever want my abilities to be context-contingent: I always want to know I have the power to create wherever, whenever and whatever the circumstances. My approach reinforces that. But if I had to write in an office, I could. I just wouldn't choose it.

LEARNING WHAT WORKS FOR YOU

I don't like to feel isolated, so I usually write in busy places with my laptop. I'll work anywhere — hotel lobbies, coffee shops, bookstores — and I'll put headphones on and just write amongst people. I love working to music; give me a great hip hop mix and I can write for hours. I love the freedom of this career, and I use that freedom as a part of my process. I thrive on it, but have the ability to reign it in and generate concrete, timely results if I need to. Somebody once said to me, "Hard work is for people without talent," but I think you need both. You need talent, but you still have to know what lights you up and will get your butt in front of the computer whether there's a paycheck involved or not. I do know the more I write, the easier it is to write. The less I write, the longer it can take to start the car. I mess up all the time, I fall into patterns and struggle to stay conscious, integrated and connected, but I've learned to relish the harder stuff for the clarity that follows.

I hope this process leads you straight into the heart of your greatest asset: you. That's why I'm calling this the B-ME Method. Because I wanna be me. I want you to be you. And I believe we all create better work when we are being true to ourselves. Just be you. Or just yell: *"I gotta B-ME!"*

CHAPTER THREE

The B-ME Method

INT. WHITE VOID

A BLACK SHARPIE of the word OUTLINE materializing on a WHITE
BOARD. CARTOON OUTLINE version of Jess pops onto white void.

>   JESS
> As you just learned, the B-ME
> Method stands for the beginning,
> middle and end. And for bringing
> your real self to whatever you are
> making.

CARTOON OUTLINE CRICKETS spring on, serenading Jess as she
looks around. CARTOON TRAIN chugs into frame, doors opening
for Cartoon Jess and she hops on --

INT. FLOW TRAIN - MOMENTS LATER

-- reclining in a beautiful chaise, this might be the luxest
train-to-nowhere ever production-designed.

>   JESS
> Whether you decide to write a
> script, a presentation, a book or a
> talk, thinking in terms of those
> three phases can really help.
> Obvious as that sounds.

Jess lifts a copy of TRAVEL MAGAZINE, featuring A PICTURE OF
HERSELF ON A CHAISE ON A TRAIN. A nearby PASSENGER shaking
their head in disapproval.

>   JESS (CONT'D)
>   (to Passenger)
> If they can make SNAKES ON A PLANE,
> I can make CHAISE ON A TRAIN.
>   (to camera)
> I encourage you to figure out a way
> to push through inner disapproval
> and silence the judgement. First
> rule of B-ME is to be you.

Annoyed, the Passenger moves to a seat that is farther away.

>   JESS (CONT'D)
> You will judge you. The imaginary
> passengers in your mind may throw
> shade. It's normal.
>   (MORE)

> JESS (CONT'D)
> You'll likely encounter all of this
> and more on the way to your
> destination: the end of your
> outline.

ZOOMING into the magazine cover, featuring ENDLESS Jess'
holding ENDLESS copies of the same magazine.

> JESS (CONT'D)
> It can feel endless, I know. But
> it's not!

CLOSE ON: BLUE RECYCLING BIN

Dizzy, Jess opens a BLUE RECYCLING BIN. SOUNDS of APPLAUSE.
Alarmed, she slams the lid. Opens. APPLAUSE.

> JESS
> Try to quiet that critical voice
> and trust. Trust your <u>inner</u>
> applause meter. This is what you
> want to cozy up to - even if it
> leads you through some weird
> places.

With that, Jess puts her head into the. Then her whole body.
The unseen CROWD GOES WILD.

INT. ENDLESS RECYLING BIN TUNNEL - MOMENTS LATER

Crawling towards us, Jess pushes aside CANS and BOTTLES.

> JESS
> I don't recommend outer applause-
> seeking. But once you have
> connected with your idea and commit
> to your creative journey, you may
> reach a point where you have to
> trot it out for air and take it for
> a spin. For other humans.

Behind her, a FIRE explodes. She lifts a GIANT LID and steps
out of a DUMPSTER FIRE and onto --

EXT. HOLLYWOOD BACKLOT - DAY

-- A STUDIO BACKLOT! Brushing embers off her smoking
clothing, Jess dodges GOLF CARTS and GAFFERS as she is
checked in by a SECURITY GUARD.

                    JESS
          As I was first navigating
          Hollywood, I had to start from
          scratch. In a very old car without
          air conditioning --

The Guard's studying her Driver's License before handing her
a DRIVE-ON PASS.

                    JESS (CONT'D)
          -- selling what was then called
          CHEER FEVER. This involved pitching
          my idea to studio executives and
          producers.

SUPER QUICK CUTS of 27 MORE SECURITY GUARDS and DRIVE-ON
PASSES.

                    JESS (CONT'D)
          Once. Or twice. Or maybe twenty-
          something times. That's right. I
          pitched CHEER FEVER twenty eight
          times and got twenty seven NOs. But
          who's counting?

Jess waving a STUDIO DRIVE-ON PASS out the window.

                    JESS (CONT'D)
          That's what starting from scratch
          looked like in August of 1996!
          Without cell phones.

OVERHEAD SHOT of Jess. Drenched with exhaustion.

                    JESS (CONT'D)
          In honor of that endless series of
          meetings, I'd like to share the
          'Written-For-The-Spoken-Word
          Version of the Official Original
          Pitch Outline for CHEER FEVER.' ©
          Copyright Jessica Bendinger, the
          Mother of Bring It On.

Jess curtsies, lowering her head all the way to the floor,
then turning to WINK.

                    JESS (CONT'D)
          Also known as the pitch for BRING
          IT ON. By all means feel free to
          skip ahead and check it out in
          Chapter Nine. If you wanna really
          get into character, please try
          performing it aloud, in 102 degree
          heat.
                    (MORE)

                    JESS (CONT'D)
Preferably after driving in a car
with no A/C. In Hollywood. In
August. Otherwise, enjoy this next
section of The Playbook. All tools.
No rules.

CHAPTER FOUR

The Triple Treats

Sides. Guides. Rides.

INT. TROPHY ROOM - DAY

CLOSE ON: TROPHY CASE

QUICK CUTS OF EGOT: EMMY, GRAMMY, OSCAR and TONY's, PALME
D'ORS, GOLDEN GLOBES, BAFTAS, PEOPLE'S CHOICE, TEEN CHOICE,
MTV VMAS, OLYMPIC MEDALS, PULITZERS, NOBELS and some GIRL
SCOUT BADGES.

Jess in GIRL SCOUT gear toasting marshmallows over a fire.

>   JESS
>   I wrote about the B-ME technique in
>   the early aughts. So you can
>   imagine my surprise when Barry
>   Jenkins won the Oscar for MOONLIGHT
>   and subsequently credited this
>   technique? I was super flattered.
>   (flattered)
>   I was very, very stoked for him.
>   Rules prevent me from disclosing my
>   vote. And vanity forces me to share
>   this here.

WIDER reveals Jess' bonfire built upon flaming OSCARS. Wink.

INT. THRONE ROOM - NIGHT

Jess quietly stroking a rare BORNEO CLOUDED LEOPARD.

>   JESS
>   So, here we are. It's the twenty
>   first century. Many, many books on
>   screenwriting exist. Which is
>   great. In thirty years, the section
>   has exploded.
>   (yawning)
>   But it still bores the spit outta
>   me.

Jess lifting and wielding a SCEPTER.

>   JESS (CONT'D)
>   There's still no magic wand or
>   magic scepter.
>   (MORE)

> JESS (CONT'D)
> But that doesn't stop proponents of
> techniques from sounding imperial.
> Regal. Or absolute. As if
> screenwriting rules descended from
> on high.
> (burping adorably)
> So, I'm thinking -- you know, it's
> 2020. We're all inside wearing
> masks, so why not toss my two cents
> into the ring?

She snaps, transforming the scepter into an apron out of thin
air, draping it around her own neck.

> JESS (CONT'D)
> Think of this section as containing
> some no-rules tools to keep or
> toss. I like to think of writing as
> a form of play, so these are ways I
> like to gamify my storytelling.
> Shall we?

EXT. HIGHWAY

Jess is driving in a convertible, pointing.

> JESS
> As I mentioned, I hate rules. But I
> love help. Useful suggestions.
> (yelling)
> The Triple Treats.

FREEWAY splits into THREE DIVERGENT LANES.

> JESS (CONT'D)
> I'm calling them Triple Treats
> instead of Triple Threats.

RISING, wielding a samurai SWORD a la KILL BILL, whilst
driving with her FEET.

> JESS (CONT'D)
> If you respond better to
> malevolence than benevolence, feel
> free to add an 'H' and turn the
> 'treat' into a 'threat.'

She hurls the sword out of the moving car.

ON SWORD: SLO-MO through the air...cutting PINEAPPLES...into
beautifully carved pieces, landing...ON AN AIRBORNE PLATE.

                    JESS (CONT'D)
                 (helicopter sound)
           If you are aware of the triple
           treats, it can help you feel
           less...lost. Not entirely but maybe
           they can rescue your perspective.

HELICOPTER lowering a ladder, Jess grabs a RUNG.

                    JESS (CONT'D)
           The triple treats go like this.
                 (eating pineapple)
           Three Sides. Three Guides. Three
           Rides.

The chopper begins moving, as Jess barely hangs onto the
ladder. Passing BILLBOARD reading: THREE SIDES

                    JESS (CONT'D)
           Let's start with the Three Sides.
           Why? Because I said so, that's
           why.

Jess continues ascending the ladder and now holds onto the
landing SKID.

                    JESS (CONT'D)
           There are 'three sides' to every
           story. If you enjoy shapes? Picture
           a circle.

A nearby SKYWRITER makes a CIRCLE with A DOT inside.

                    JESS (CONT'D)
           Your character is the dot in the
           center. If the circumference is 360
           degrees, each degree is a *possible*
           story line. So it's more like
           three hundred and sixty sides to
           every story, but let's keep it
           simple for now. 'Sides' are a way
           to keep point-of-view alive. Or --

UAP shaped like a TRIANGLE radiating GREEN LIGHT.

                    JESS (CONT'D)
           Picture a triangle. Three sides to
           narrative that might include: A
           Hero. A Victim. A Villain.
           Psychology refers to this as The
           Dreaded Drama Triangle or the
           Karpman Drama Triangle.

Jess waves hello to the alien craft. An FRIENDLY ALIEN pops out, waving back.

>   JESS (CONT'D)
>   Invert that idea and you get its'
>   healthier counterpart: The
>   Empowerment Dynamic. This includes:
>   The Challenger. The Creator. The
>   Coach. Much has been written about
>   this by folks much smarter than I
>   am. It's very helpful for those of
>   you who want extra credit. Check
>   it out. It's a way of imagining
>   outcomes and scenarios using well-
>   known, well-worn dynamics. A
>   framework.

A HAND pulling Jess up into the helicopter, strapping PARACHUTE PACK onto her back.

>   JESS (CONT'D)
>   I believe there are also 'Three
>   Guides' to consider while imagining
>   or elaborating on a project.

MID-AIR CHOPPER LADDER MONTAGE: QUICK CUTS

- holding an APPLE in one hand and a STUFFED APPLE TOY in the other.

>   JESS (CONT'D)
>   The quality.
>   (biting real apple)
>   What's the vibe? Is it genuine?
>   Realistic?
>   (sniffing toy)
>   Or is it weird? Silly or cartoony?

- balancing a GRANDFATHER CLOCK and a STOPWATCH.

>   JESS (CONT'D)
>   The timing. Is it a short? Is it
>   six seasons? Or ninety minutes?

- opening a CASH REGISTER grabbing PENNIES and STACKS of HUNDREDS.

>   JESS (CONT'D)
>   And the cost of the thing you are
>   imagining or developing. Is there
>   no budget? Low budget? Faux budget?

WIDER on Jess CATAPULTING the APPLES, CLOCKS and CASH REGISTER onto different points on TRIANGLE.

                    JESS (CONT'D)
          MBA's refer to this as the project
          management triangle.

                    CHOPPER SPEAKER (O.S.)
          I think you mean: Good. Fast.
          Cheap. Pick two.

TOM CRUISE *IN MY MIND* appearing, hanging from another
helicopter.

                    TOM CRUISE
          What if I want to control all
          three?

                    JESS
               (to camera)
          If you're Tom Cruise, you might
          actually be able to control all
          three.
               (smiling, to Tom)
          Thanks, Tom!

                    TOM CRUISE
          My pleasure. You might want to
          rewrite this without chopper noise.

                    JESS
               (unable to hear)
          You think I'm smart? That's so
          nice!
               (yelling louder)
          Can you explain how the project
          management triangle works? Maybe
          while doing some aerial stunts?

Giving a thumbs up, Tom releases from the skid, doing AERIAL
stunts as we fall with him. His chest reads the word: GOOD!
As TWO MORE SKYDIVERS (we'll call them FAST! and CHEAP!) join
Tom.

                    TOM CRUISE
          Good, fast, cheap. Pick two.

Tom links with FAST. Pushing CHEAP away.

                    TOM CRUISE (CONT'D)
          Good and fast isn't cheap.

FAST! and CHEAP! linking. Shoving Tom out of it.

                    TOM CRUISE (CONT'D)
          Cheap and fast isn't good.
               (winking)
                    (MORE)

>   TOM CRUISE (CONT'D)
> But if I'm not in it? How could it
> be?

CHEAP! Corralling Tom so their chests read: GOOD + CHEAP.

>   TOM CRUISE (CONT'D)
> And good and cheap?

FAST! Now mock-crying from being left out.

>   TOM CRUISE (CONT'D)
> Good and cheap is usually _not_ fast.

Deploying his parachute, Tom yanking upwards. Jess falls past him, her parachute not opening. TIME SLOWS.

>   JESS
> Rules to live by and create by. If
> you can grab all three, grab away,
> Grabbycakes!

A GREEN SCREEN illuminating behind her, Jess is actually fake-flailing on an APPLE BOX --

INT. SOUNDSTAGE - CONTINUOUS

-- as someone yells "CUT!" as STUNT COORDINATORS help her out of this position and GRIPS move gear.

>   JESS
> This last treat is called the
> 'three rides.' It refers to the
> process of progressing that thing
> you are imagining, writing and
> making. The version you write. The
> version you shoot or make. The
> version you edit.

>   STUNT COORDINATOR
> What if you're just writing?

>   JESS
> That's a dangerous question. Are
> you licensed to ask that?

>   STUNT COORDINATOR
> Yes. Danger is my business.

>   JESS
> If you have a healthy relationship
> with your mother, I will answer
> that.

                    STUNT COORDINATOR
          I'm an orphan.

                    JESS
          Nice try.

                    STUNT COORDINATOR
          My mother is alive. The point is, I
          can't write about it because I'm
          paralyzed with fear of the blank
          page. It's really scary.

                    JESS
          I get it. Just remember: three
          rides. The one you imagine or
          outline. The one you generate and
          write or make. And the one you
          really hone in on as you rewrite
          and polish and finish.

                    STUNT COORDINATOR
          Three??? But what if it's perfect
          when it comes out?

                    JESS
          Everyone thinks it's perfect. It
          rarely is. I'm so sorry. Three
          steps. It'll go by quick but you
          gotta get over your resistance.

                    STUNT COORDINATOR
          That's a very long way of saying
          'it's a process'! Are you saying
          there's a beginning, middle and end
          for everything?

                    JESS
          Yup. Let's look at your script.

Sitting down, ANGLE ON: SCRIPT

We ZOOM into the text so it's full frame.

*JESS AND TOM begin KISSING PASSIONATELY WHILE DESCENDING to
earth in TANDEM PARACHUTES.*

                    JESS (CONT'D)
          I outlined this as an action-
          adventure sequence with a touch of
          romance. That was the first ride.
          The version I dreamed up and wrote.

A GIANT BOBBLE-HEAD of Tom Cruise appears on a FLUFFY DOG BODY. Walking on its' hind legs.

> STUNT COORDINATOR
> (confused)
> Is that a Pomeranian? Wearing a Tom Cruise bobble-head?

> JESS
> The production could only afford a comedy sequence featuring Pom Cruise, the hottest new dog influencer since...anyway, that's the version we shot.

POM CRUISE barks adorably. THE IMAGE FREEZES.

ANGLE ON old school 35MM footage REWINDING through the "frames" as an UNSEEN EDITOR splices the celluloid.

> JESS (CONT'D)
> The editor cut that out entirely. Because puns are fun to read, but are much harder to pull off. That's the version you edit.

COVER OF *DOG FANCY* Magazine slapping full screen. Headline reads: *POM CRUISE sweeps Westminster!*

> EDITOR
> This joke still isn't working. I'm gonna remove it from this scene completely, let me know if you miss it.

ON JESSICA, wiping a tear from her eye.

> JESS
> I rarely miss it! What's wrong with me???

> EDITOR
> By the way, no one cuts on film anymore.

BACK TO REALITY, where Jess rides atop a crane.

> JESS
> There's the project you imagine, outline and write. If it's a script, there's the pages you write. The movie you shoot. And the movie you edit. Three different rides!

Jess jumping off the crane, landing on the seat of a DUCATI. Whipping on a HELMET with ease.

                    JESS (CONT'D)
          Time for a recap.

THE TRIPLE TREATS

THREE SIDES: ORIENTATION

Writers are juggling multiple perspectives at once:

1) what the writer experiences making the story

2) what the hero experiences inside the story

3) what the audience experiences AKA the story itself

It can be confusing. Be gentle as you expand this capacity to orient yourself and zoom in, zoom out and around your work.

For further study around understanding psychologicalinterplay and character interaction, check out:

KARPMAN DRAMA TRIANGLE - Stephen Karpman refined this frame around identity dynamics. The Hero/Rescuer; The Victim; The Villain/Persecutor.

THE EMPOWERMENT DYNAMIC - shifts these roles into more 'empowered' positions on the triangle: The Teacher/Coach; The Creator/Survivor; The Challenger.

Mind-mapping, path-finding and trajectory projection are critical skills in storytelling and world-building. Why? You have to start imagining and experimenting and expanding into your next best version. Of yourself. Of your writing. Of your desired outcomes and your connection to all those things. That takes patience and practice. And more patience and more practice.

THREE GUIDES: PARAMETERS

There are three guideposts to help frame process when you're overwhelmed or lost:

1) GOOD = the quality

2) FAST = the timing

3) CHEAP = the budget/cost/resources

THE PROJECT MANAGEMENT TRIANGLE - Unless you are Tom Clancy and writing novels...or Tom Cruise and budget is no object, these factors influence every project. Especially if you are feeling out of control or like you need a help reigning it in.

THREE RIDES: VARIETY

Like the beginning, middle and end of an outline, there are often three macro phases to every creative process.

1) YOUR FIRST RIDE: <u>The thing you imagine</u>. The perfect abstraction. Pure ideation and creation. If a screenplay is your final goal, the first ride will the outline. When a movie is the final goal, I call the screenplay the first ride.

2)YOUR NEXT RIDE: <u>The thing you make</u>. What you commit and recommit time, energy or resources to. You've figured things out. You know your way around a little better. If it's a screenplay, this will be your first, second or third draft. If it's TV pilot, for example, it may be the version of the script you shoot.

3)YOUR LAST HURRAH: <u>The thing you review, rework, revise</u>. This is your final screenplay, novel, podcast once it is cut, shined and polished. It's the final product of all your hard work, and can look very different from the perfect abstraction inside your mind.

Three different rides. Make friends with them versus demanding perfection out of them. Do you like people who demand perfection out of you without anything in return? Me neither. Don't do that to yourself.

There's no such thing as a happy ending to a miserable journey. I'm working on becoming someone who is really good at enjoying the process. I'm still working on it.

CHAPTER FIVE

The Three C's

Content. Context. Culture.

INT. OPEN ROAD - DAY

THREE DRONES blazing by Jess, blowing hair into her lip-glossed mouth.

> JESS
> You think I'd be --
> (spitting hair)
> -- more glamorous in my own
> screenwriting, outlining HOW-TO.
> But no. As I've said, just my
> opinion. Not scripture. Not dogma.
> Quite possibly hooey.

WIDER reveals she is sprawled on top of a giant PILE of HOOEY.

> JESS (CONT'D)
> I don't know what hooey is, so use
> your imagination. Try not to be
> gross.

BACK TO JESS pointing to A BILLBOARD.

The THREE C'S

> JESS (CONT'D)
> I'm a licensed script doctor. Board
> certified in fifty-nine states.
> (then)
> Other places besides America have
> states. State of Indifference?
> State of Grace? Don't judge me for
> that joke. Comedy is bloody.

INT. UCLA CLASSROOM

Jessica's arms are bloody for no visible reason, but the BRUIN STUDENTS are too engaged on phones to notice.

> JESS
> When I taught a graduate
> screenwriting class at UCLA. I
> wanted something efficient <u>and</u>
> effective. Basically?
> (MORE)

                    JESS (CONT'D)
            This is the book I wish I'd had.
            That didn't exist. Til now.

INT. TELEVISION SET

PAT SAJAK onscreen. But he sounds like JESS.

                    PAT SAJAK
            Content is King. But context is
            god. And Culture is the cradle
            they're both rocking in. What the
            heck do I mean?

WHEEL OF FORTUNE's VANNA WHITE flipping over six more letters
that spell CONTENT. Jess is now a contestant.

                    JESS
            The content! The story!
            Specifically, whatever you make
            with the outline technique I
            mentioned a few pages ago.

                    PAT SAJAK
            You mentioned this already.

                    JESS
            Thanks for mentioning that I just
            mentioned the mention. Super
            helpful. I'd like to buy one letter
            and that letter is --
                    (screaming)
            I'd like to buy an X!

The "N" changes to an "X," turning the word to CONTEXT.

                    JESS (CONT'D)
            We all know the word CONTEXT. And
            with anything you make, you gotta
            know **what** you are making.

ZOOM INTO monitor...becoming an old-school B+W TV, as two
1950's TEENS are googly-eyeing each other.

                    JESS (CONT'D)
            Is it an old-fashioned TV show
            about teens in search of love?

ZOOM WIDER to reveal the image is now on Jess's PHONE. In her
other hand, a COMIC BOOK covered in CHEF'S HATS.

                    JESS (CONT'D)
            Or is it a comic book about chefs
            chasing elusive ingredients?

Jess throws the COMIC BOOK against the wall and it becomes a
LAPTOP SCREEN featuring --

                    JESS (CONT'D)
               Is it a vlog about vampires in
               search of renewable blood sources?
               In Holland?

-- TWO VAMPIRES swinging their cloaks, revealing insane
CLOGGING step abilities.

                    JESS (CONT'D)
                 (sheepishly)
               Vampires in clogs making vlogs?

Spinning around, revealing she's wearing a VAMPIRE CLOAK.
Lifting her arm to shield herself from the FOOTLIGHT -- ON A
STAGE! In front of an AUDIENCE of mainly OLDER MEN in similar
fleece jackets and vests.

                    JESS (CONT'D)
               Or is it a TED talk --

REVERSE reveals Jess in front of giant red TED letters,
holding a Power Point clicker and wearing plastic CLOGS.

                    JESS (CONT'D)
               -- about people addicted to TED
               talks?

Behind her, IMAGES of a TV, a PHONE SCREEN, a COMIC BOOK, a
LAPTOP SCREEN, a TED stage illuminate as she talks.

                    JESS (CONT'D)
               This is your context.
                 (pausing thoughtfully)
               It is the 'what it is.'
               The very zoomed-out arena of your
               idea.

EXT. BAKER LIBRARY - HARVARD BUSINESS SCHOOL - DAY

At the GRADUATION PODIUM, Jess gives the Commencement Speech.

                    JESS
               The third C is -- CULTURE.
               Why am I telling you this at
               Harvard? I though you guys knew
               everything already --

Moving the tassel on the graduation cap, she exits stage, met
by the GHOST of PETER DRUCKER -- the Godfather of modern
business strategy -- joining this stroll.

> PETER DRUCKER
> Because you got the idea from me,
> Peter Drucker, one of the best-
> known and most widely influential
> thinkers and writers on the subject
> of management theory and practice.

> JESS
> It's true. Peter, please share the
> quote.

> PETER DRUCKER
> 'Culture eats strategy for
> breakfast.'

> JESS
> Yes! Content is King but Context is
> God. And Culture eats strategy for
> breakfast.
> (bowing to Mr. Drucker)
> Peter Drucker - take it away!

The Ghost of Peter Drucker™ rising, looming over us.

> PETER DRUCKER
> The culture itself - the world at
> large - will be a factor. If you
> don't acknowledge this, it might
> eat your plans. These three things
> need to be aligned and enabling
> each other, as you know from trying
> to be a female writer-director in a
> business rife with internalized
> misogyny.

POV Reaching for the camera, pulling it INTO HIS MOUTH, we
are being chewed by The Ghost of Peter Drucker™

INT. PETER DRUCKER COMMAND CENTER - BLACKBOARD

SCIENTISTS and ENGINEERS anxiously poised around a giant
SAFE. Jess puts a STETHOSCOPE up to the safe, listening and
trying to crack the code.

> JESS
> So internalized misogyny is real!
> I knew it! Incoming!

The Ghost of Peter Drucker™ is back, wearing a Tasteful Ghost
Mumu™.

>   PETER DRUCKER
> Not only were you a woman but you
> were a woman writing about young
> women. Double whammy. Even though
> your movies made the studios tons
> of money. Tons of money for an
> indifferent business ruled by
> frustrated and infantalized man-
> children. Who confuse strong women
> with scolding mothers or wives. And
> don't think women go to movies.
> Because they're not women.

The safe OPENS! They cracked it. The team begins filling
DUFFLE BAGS with MONEY.

>   PETER DRUCKER (CONT'D)
> Let's not excuse all the women with
> their own cases of unhealed,
> internalized misogyny.
> Unfortunately, they are usually
> worse than the men. I know that's
> not politically correct. I'm sorry.
> I wish you'd called me sooner --

>   JESS
> No, no, it's only two decades late,
> but very helpful, thank you. I
> think --

>   PETER DRUCKER
> I think it's nice that you're not
> canceling or shaming everyone
> guilty of this, by the way. Very
> honorable IMO and TBH as the kids
> would say. You're in. Go!

Jess slowly drawing three concentric circles on the
whiteboard as if slowing down will help.

>   JESS
> Okay. There's the world of your
> story: the arena.
>   (drawing smaller circle
>   inside 1st circle)
> There's the world inside your
> story: your characters, your plot.
>   (drawing bigger circle
>   around 1st circle)
> Then there's the world outside your
> story: the audience. The culture.

                    PETER DRUCKER (O.S.)
          The content. The context. The
          culture. That's good, actually.

                    JESS
          Thank you! See? Peter Drucker
          agrees with me in my mind.

                    PETER DRUCKER
          I am you in your mind.

Jess does a perfect Herkie jump.

                    JESS
          Why is this important? This is a
          practical consideration for any
          writer or creator. Any storyteller,
          to be honest. Which is anyone
          telling or selling anything, IMHO.

EXT. SIX FLAGS SCREENWRITING PARK

Jess is riding up the roller coaster hill alone.

                    JESS
          I want you to look deeply at your
          motives.

She raises her hands at the top, screaming.

                    JESS (CONT'D)
          EXACTLY WHY ARE YOU MAKING <u>THIS</u>
          THING FOR <u>THIS</u> AUDIENCE?

SCREECH. The car STOPS. At the top. Getting out, Jess runs
and leaps off the edge, flying through the air.

                    JESS (CONT'D)
          You can make it for fun and play,
          that's fine. You can make it
          because you absolutely must create
          it, also fine. You can explore this
          because you want to understand
          something about yourself or the
          world. All fine.

Pulling a string, a PARACHUTE jerking Jess into the air.

                    JESS (CONT'D)
          But remember, once you decide that
          you are making this for an
          audience, it is important to
          understand your audience.
                    (MORE)

                    JESS (CONT'D)
          Even if it's you.
               (floating peacefully)
          Your audience does not exist in a
          vacuum.

A GIANT VACUUM appears above Jess from the heavens, sucking
her and the parachute into it.

INT. GIANT VACUUM

Jess is landing comfortably on a bed of lint and animal hair.

                    JESS
          Nature abhors a vacuum.
               (whispering)
          Personally, I like vacuums but they
          are not great for getting your work
          out there. To an actual audience.

CLOSE UP on Jess, using a stray broken LEGO piece in the
dusty chamber as a stool. TWO LINT BALLS eat smaller lint
balls. But in a cute totally not cannibalistic way.

                    JESS (CONT'D)
          Basically, 'culture' and 'audience'
          is NOT a dirty word. It's an
          important reminder: don't phone it
          in --

WIDER reveals she's in a VACUUM CANISTER, SCREAMING. No one
can hear her scream. Giving up, Jess holds up a SIGN.

SIGN READS: ***DON'T PHONE IT IN FROM YOUR BUBBLE. IMAGINE IT IN
THE WORLD!***

                    JESS (CONT'D)
               (reading sign)
          -- don't phone it in from your
          bubble. Imagine it in the world.
          Here we come, World!

Jess kicking open the canister siding and jumping out. She is
covered in vacuum detritus.

                    JESS (CONT'D)
          But remember: Hollywood is a old
          fashioned business. If they'd
          modernized more quickly, they would
          be streaming platforms instead of
          working for them. If power were in
          the right place, creators with real
          stats might have the money and
          decision-making power.

CORONAS of LIGHT emerging. CROWN and SASH magically land upon head and shoulders. Sash reading: *QUEEN DATA SUPERNOVA*

> JESS (CONT'D)
> Not gatekeepers, agents or middle
> men with nice cars and very little
> skin in the game. Think about it.
> We need to remake this shindig for
> stakeholders. And reward those
> who've delivered more than gates
> and middles?
> > (catching bouquets)
> Happy to unpack this, this
> conundrum. Hollywood's in
> transition. Let me know who wants
> to build a more profitable, more
> inclusive future.

THREE C's: CONTENT, CONTEXT, CULTURE

When you are ready to drill into what it is, the what it's about and who it's for, you're building bridges.

1) THE CONTENT: The what it is.

2) THE CONTEXT: The what it's about.

3) THE CULTURE: The world <u>outside</u> your story. AKA The Audience.

This is Jedi-level stuff, but I'm putting it here. Artists who think about audiences aren't less artistic. They might just be pragmatic. I like to think about who I am making this for and what their world is like. It is not being a sell-out. It's being dialed in, and that is super a-ok with me.

CHAPTER SIX

The Three T's:
Theme. Tone. Twist.

EXT. PLANET EARTH - DAY

A RED CURTAIN falls over the BLUE MARBLE. A HAND emerges
holding a bottle of HOT SAUCE. The other hand holding a copy
of THE TIPPING POINT.

> JESS
> Speaking of culture, I thought I'd
> invoke one of the world's leading
> experts --

> MALCOLM GLADWELL (O.S.)
> Are you going to invoke threes
> again?

> JESS
> Yes, Malcolm Gladwell of my mind, I
> am. What are you bringing into the
> mix that has never --
> (coy)
> 'been brought' -- before? Like you
> do in your books? And podcasts?

MALCOLM GLADWELL IN MY MIND appears. He ignores Jess.

> MALCOLM GLADWELL
> Jessica adapted my seminal New
> Yorker article, 'THE COOL HUNT' for
> the screen. As she frequently
> reminds people.
> (long pause, to camera)
> You'll note there's no movie by
> that name.

Standing in the awkward silence. Neither speaks.

> JESS
> I one hundred percent apologize. I
> wanted COOL HUNT: THE MOVIE, too.

> MALCOLM GLADWELL
> Me, three. I know how you enjoy
> those.

> JESS
> Hopefully, your consecutive decades
> on the best-seller list have eased
> the sting.
> (MORE)

                    JESS (CONT'D)
Can I get back to my book now? Or
should we promote your benevolent
empire?

                    MALCOLM GLADWELL
Proceed.

                    JESS
Socioeconomic inequality and
cultural appropriation in
cheerleading skirts? That was the
Theme. That was the medicine in the
candy.

                    MALCOLM GLADWELL
Doing it through mouthy teenage
girls who spoke like gay men, that
was the Tone. But I am in your mind
until my office sends a cease and
desist --

                    JESS
What was the Twist?

                    MALCOLM GLADWELL
Cheerleading + hip hop? Those were
two great tastes that tasted great
together. I'd never actually seen
the two things together, but it
worked. That was the twist. It's
creative cross-pollination. Call it
whatever you want --

                    JESS
        (to camera)
Two great tastes that taste great
together? Malcolm Gladwell and my
twist chapter. C'mon.

                    MALCOLM GLADWELL
A bit on the nose for my taste.

INT. NON-TRADEMARKED OLYMPIC RINGS - NIGHT

QUICK CUTS of ELF, BRIDESMAIDS, DEADPOOL, BREAKING BAD, GAME
OF THRONES and any and every breakout hit appearing inside
the non-trademarked rings.

                    JESS
So. What is that new, slightly
unfamiliar concept being
transplanted into your material?
        (MORE)

JESS (CONT'D)
This unlikely thing that will give
it the combinatorial power of a new
thing. Healthy cross-fertilization.
Creative transplanting. The twist.
New hybrids and new art. It's the
element of surprise - the familiar
with the unfamiliar - that will
give what you make OOMPH.
Relevance. Freshness.

THREE T'S: THEME, TONE, TWIST

Ingredients you might want to play with as you are searching
for your creative identity and your unique voice.
Suggestions for exploration include:

1) THE THEME

- What is the underlying/overall message of your story?

- What are you really talking about?

- What's a problem you're trying to understand, solve or
highlight?

2) THE TONE

- How is your story going to be told? Comedically?
Dramatically? Mysteriously?

- What is unusual or fresh about how you're doing this?

3) THE TWIST

- What is your unfamiliar element?

- What's being transplanted into your material, making it
fresh?

CHAPTER SEVEN

The Three P's:

POV, Polarity, Play

EXT. EMPTY DESERT - NIGHT

Jess looking around for inspiration. MOON rising.

> JESS
> Selling BRING IT ON took commitment
> to a point-of-view. My POV was that
> I believed the sidelines belonged
> front and center. It seems obvious
> now, but it wasn't. I took the
> sidelines very seriously.

Looking up to the skies, stretching out her arms.

> JESS (CONT'D)
> Why? Because I totally related to
> feeling sidelined and
> underestimated.

She HOWLS. LIGHTNING STRIKES nearby.

> JESS (CONT'D)
> You have to claim the unique things
> you take seriously.
> (dodging a lightning bolt)
> Point of view is about screaming
> and leaning into what you are
> curious about. And owning it.

INT. EMPTY LIBRARY - NIGHT

She is wandering around, alone.

> JESS (CONT'D)
> There may be no one else there. You
> may have to go there alone. All by
> yourself. It's okay.

Approaching shelf after shelf of BOOKS.

> JESS (CONT'D)
> Don't despair. Pay attention.
> Because if you follow your
> curiosity, and - this is tricky -
> notice where others disagree. Where
> do they disagree with you? Either
> in the world or in your head?
> (MORE)

                    JESS (CONT'D)
          That's energy. That's polarity. And
          that tension can fuel the creative
          legions inside you. It can be the
          music you dance with on the page,
          proving your point in imaginative
          ways. Let it charge you up. Let
          the energy - whatever it is - let
          it pull you in and have its' way
          with you. Let it ping around inside
          and stir you up. Let it make you
          question stuff.

Pulling out a BOOK, revealing a PORTAL, that sucks her in.

INT. AURORA BOREALIS - MAGIC HOUR

Jess exiting out of a magical igloo under a GREENLIT sky.

                    JESS
          Or maybe you need to invoke a
          magical mentor who has what you
          think you need. Like I've been
          doing this entire book --

The KATY PERRY *IN MY MIND* appearing above the igloo in a out-
of-this-world gardening outfit. Snapping a GLASS STRUCTURE --

INT. GREENHOUSE - CONTINUOUS

-- a GREENHOUSE (!) around Katy and Jess.

                    JESS (CONT'D)
          Katy Perry, for example. She's fun.
          She's magical. She's PLAYFUL.
          That's what I need when I take
          myself or my ideas too seriously. I
          need to remember to play.

Katy SNAPS; Jess magically floating...her face contorting
with a little fear.

                    JESS (CONT'D)
          I can't remember why I brought you
          here -- this feels unhinged. And,
          well, floaty.

                    KATY PERRY
          This is the part where you take
          everything you've outlined. Shade
          in your theme, your tone and your
          twist - and invest in your point of
          view. You may feel untethered and
          uncertain --

Katy SNAPS again. Jess lands on the ground with a THUD.

> KATY PERRY (CONT'D)
> Or clunky and thud-like. But this
> is creativity. Investing in and
> nurturing the thing you are
> exploring and growing, whatever it
> is. Try it in song. Or rhyme.

Jess is SINGING to the plants with Katy and DANCING.

> JESS
> Don't know what it's about? Try
> 'Dancing it out'?
> When I'm filled with dread, it gets
> me out of my head -- ?

Jess is shimmying inside the greenhouse with abandon.

> JESS (CONT'D)
> (looking around)
> Katy? Where'd you go? Oh no! Here
> they come --

OUTSIDE THE GREENHOUSE, we watch as Jess is suddenly alone
and locked in, her HANDS and FACE pressing against the glass.

> JESS (CONT'D)
> 'Why did I start writing this?'
> 'Who do I think I am?'
> 'Who on earth will give a toss?'
> 'I have no recollection of who this
> is for!'
> 'What is going on? Am I losing it?'
> 'Why am I writing myself as trapped
> inside an imaginary greenhouse!
> Abandoned by Katy Perry?'

OUTSIDE OPRAH *IN MY MIND* is strolling by with BRENE BROWN *IN
MY MIND*, laughing and talking...not seeing Jess pounding on
the glass.

> JESS (CONT'D)
> Will I ever meet Oprah? Or Brene
> Brown? Is my Super Soul, super-
> sized? Am I Daring Greatly or
> Rising Strong..ly?

Then, LIZ GILBERT *IN MY MIND* and CHERYL STRAYED *IN MY MIND*
sauntering up to Oprah and Brene under Oprah's oak trees.

> JESS (CONT'D)
> Will my Eating, Praying and Loving
> ever turn into Big Magic?
> (MORE)

                    JESS (CONT'D)
               (knocking)
          Will my Tiny Beautiful Sugar ever
          be Untamed?

WRITER GLENNON DOYLE (*in Jess's mind*), strolls by. Exhausted,
Jess sits on the greenhouse floor.

                    JESS (CONT'D)
          Wait - what happened? I went from
          dancing with my fear to compare and
          despair time! AAARRRGH. Fear can be
          tricky, even when you're dancing
          with it.
          But you know why I included all
          those spectacular creative women?
          Because they know how to be
          playful, even when they're talking
          about serious stuff. They have a
          sense of humor. I want to emulate
          that. Play, play, play. Laugh. And
          if that fails, I might encourage
          you to --

She curls up on the ledge to nap, while sipping some COCOA
and holding a phone.

                    JESS (CONT'D)
          HALT! Are you hungry, angry,
          lonely, or tired? Projects and
          people need informed pause.
          Ventilation. Air. Naps. Sometimes
          all of those things. At once.
               (slurping cocoa)
          Calling best friend for some back-
          up. Tina?

                    TINA (O.S.)
          You're amazing. I love you. Keep
          going. You're the best. I'm also
          here to remind you that you always
          feel better after you meditate.

Jess pulls down a SHADE which becomes a SCREEN. MONKS
chanting OM fill the void.

EXT. GARDEN LABYRINTH - DAY

Jess pops up from meditation to stroll and meander.

                    JESS
          Consider meditation for stagnation.
          If that doesn't work for you -
               (sighs)
                    (MORE)

> JESS (CONT'D)
> - maybe take some walks.
> (pointing to a bird)
> Or just be in the world. Meander.
> Frolick.
> (Googling)
> Ask questions. Stay curious. Stay
> hungry for answers. How? By moving
> away from the intense focus and
> putting soft focus to work. Relax.
> Dance it out. Take your POV and
> give it some polarity and play.
> You'll mess up. And when you mess
> up, give these states a whirl.

THREE P'S: POV, POLARITY, PLAY

Feeling stuck is normal. Having strategies for becoming unstuck is essential. Consider trying these:

1) POINT-OF-VIEW:

- What do you really believe? Or feel? Or want to express about something?

- What bugs you? What infuriates you?

- What's that issue you are secretly (or not-so-secretly) arguing about internally?

2) POLARITY:

- If your idea drags, you may need to energize it.

- Where is the conflict? Inside of you? Between you and the world? Between your characters and the world?

- Use this energy like a battery, to fuel your flatline and animate the writing.

3) PLAY:

- Who or what makes you laugh? Drink that in when you're depleted.

- What is that song that makes you want to dance?

- When are you having fun? Do that. If you don't remember what fun is, take a nap. And then listen or watch the last thing that made you laugh. Then watch it again.

CHAPTER EIGHT

Secret Ingredient

INT. DARK ABYSS - NIGHT

Jess shines a flashlight under her chin. Not flattering.

> JESS
> Now that we've stared into the
> abyss of your creative fear, here
> are a couple techniques for dancing
> with it.

Jess points her flashlight into A CAVE. INSIDE THE CAVE, the
light illuminates a CAVE DRAWING of MIND MAP and a TIMER.

> JESS (CONT'D)
> When you feel lost in the dark of a
> new idea, please consider combining
> tools. I like mind-mapping and the
> Pomodoro method. They help break
> down the big, dark, scary parts --
> and get me from the unknowns to the
> knowns. Faster than you can say
> 'first draft.'

Jess flicks on a light, it's a beautifully decorated space
with windows, white boards and bulletin boards. INFOGRAPHIC
of Mind-Mapping.

> JESS (CONT'D)
> Many have waxed rhapsodic about
> mind-mapping. It helps me free-
> associate and meander around rough
> patches.

CIRCLES and IDEA BRANCHES blossoming to life.

> JESS (CONT'D)
> Start with an idea in a circle.
> Draw different branches and
> possible directions off that
> central idea circle. Write on those
> branches. Do offshoots. Doodle as
> long as you want - or set a timer.
> Think of this as greasing up for
> your brainstorming channels.

A giant TIMER appears on a wall.

                    JESS (CONT'D)
          The Pomodoro method keeps you on a
          schedule when you feel stuck.

TIMER reads TWENTY MINUTES.

                    JESS (CONT'D)
          So when I am stuck, this is my go-
          to secret sauce move: Twenty
          minutes. Or three pages. Whichever
          comes first.

Timer begins counting backwards.

                    JESS (CONT'D)
          If you go twenty minutes, it's a
          win. But if I can write three pages
          in less than twenty minutes, I'm a
          legend. I feel good. Participation
          trophy, please.

She dons a WORLD'S BEST GRANDPA hat.

                    JESS (CONT'D)
          If I wanna go again, I go again.
          It's this game with myself. It
          takes me out of the paralytic dread
          and into the playground. It
          gamifies the process, and lights up
          the parts of my brain that want to
          <u>win.</u>

Jess starts juggling GLOBES and TOMATOES on the unicycle.

                    JESS (CONT'D)
          Part two of the secret sauce? A
          treat. If I wanna keep going, I
          keep going. But if I want to honor
          the deal I made, I try to give
          myself a small reward.

EMMA THE DOG appears. Jess holding treats over Emma's nose,
teaching her how to spin on her hind legs.

                    JESS (CONT'D)
          I, too, will spin in circles if
          there's a reward involved.

Jess opens her sweatshirt revealing a shirt that reads: WILL
WORK FOR TREATS!

> JESS (CONT'D)
> If I want something I enjoy - a
> snack, a nap, a walk - using it as
> the reward for finishing some chunk
> of writing helps me. I am human. I
> need motivation. This works for me.
> I am able to write without doing
> this. And I can. But this makes it
> fun. It puts me in the space of
> play, and enjoying the process is
> the best secret sauce there is.
> (on one knee)
> If you are stuck, try my trick.
> Learn to hold your own hand using
> mind-maps, timers and treats. It's
> awkward at first but will become
> oddly satisfying, I promise.

INT. BUBBLE BATH - DAY

The BUBBLES are rising happily. A FACE pops out of the foam.

> JESS
> If you are lucky enough to have
> ever enjoyed a bubble bath, you
> know how delightfully predictable
> it is when bubbles foam.

A WET SCRIPT emerges from the foamy water.

> JESS (CONT'D)
> Every new writer and screenwriter
> makes the same kinds of mistakes.
> I'm gonna make this quick list as
> painless and frothy as possible.

A SOAKING WET CLOWN holding a SIGN reading TOO MANY
CHARACTERS, TOO MANY ENDINGS emerges from the bubbles.

> JESS (CONT'D)
> Sometimes we want to give important
> business to other characters. Like
> I'm doing now. Good rule of thumb:
> only add new characters unless you
> absolutely have to. Same with
> endings. I think the first draft of
> CHEER FEVER had six endings.

The Wet Clown lifts his GIANT RED SHOES out of the tub,
splashing everywhere, clomping out backwards because...big
shoes.

                         WET CLOWN
          I'm so sorry.

                           JESS
          Don't be. It's just you. No biggie.

FIVE MORE CLOWNS emerge, exiting the bathtub apologetically.

A MUFFLED WHINNY comes from under the water, announcing a
ZEBRA! Whisps of foamy goodness sticking to it.

                           ZEBRA
          Where am I? I was just in Kruger
          National Park rehearsing with my
          buddies. My teacher was telling me
          I needed to change some things --

                           JESS
          Were they asking you to do a
          rewrite?

                           ZEBRA
          I think we all know zebras don't
          change their stripes. Or their
          scripts.

                           JESS
          Zebra? May I call you Zebra?

                           ZEBRA
          The name's Don.

                           JESS
          Don. All writers have to revise
          their work -- it's part of the --

                           ZEBRA
          But this happened to me in real
          life! I'm just telling it like it
          is! This is what happened to me!
          The exact words. Exactly!

                           JESS
          I know. Let me guess: you named
          your lead character 'DON'?

                           ZEBRA
          It happened to me! And my siblings
          Danny, Debby, Donna and Duane. I'm
          trying to be honest.

                           JESS
          Listen: Don't name characters after
          yourself.
                              (MORE)

JESS (CONT'D)
Unless it's a biopic and your lead
character is famous and you happen
to share a name. Like if you were
writing the Don Juan story. You
could use Don, Don. Mix up the
names so they are easily
differentiated. Whenever possible.

Don steps outthe tub, pouting as his hooves slip on wet tile.

JESS (CONT'D)
Your readers are absorbing alot of
new information and it's a good
idea to give everyone names that
are different. A small way to be
quietly considerate of the reader.
Rewriting isn't just grammar. Or
names. It's a process.

ZEBRA
You're a bath-hole.

Don the Zebra CLIP-CLOPS away. Suddenly the SIX CLOWNS walk
back into the bathroom.

FOURTH CLOWN
We lost our keys.

FIFTH CLOWN
We were supposed to perform at a
circus --

SIXTH CLOWN
-- but we decided to make a detour
for some wrapping paper and bows --

FOURTH CLOWN
-- we need to find our keys.

The CLOWNS REENTER the tub. One hangs back.

JESS
Once you're back in there, though,
that's it. No more clown car bath.
This is it.

FIRST CLOWN
Not for you to decide.

JESS
Pick an ending guys. Leave or get
back in the tub, but you have to
commit. To one ending.

The CLOWNS look at each other, stricken.

>   THIRD CLOWN
>   We're trying to do something fresh
>   and unique and not be commercial
>   sell-outs, k? We can have as many
>   endings as we want, ok? And we
>   really don't appreciate your rules--

>   JESS
>   You can have all the endings you
>   want but unless it's a narrative
>   device that really enhances the
>   story, you'll just confuse
>   everyone. But suit yourself.

The CLOWNS GRUMBLE, disappearing back into the tub from
whence they came. The LAST CLOWN sits on the edge of the tub.

>   LAST CLOWN
>   I'm tired of being a clown in a
>   shudder of clowns.

>   JESS
>   What's a shudder of clowns?

>   LAST CLOWN
>   A group of clowns. Maybe it's why
>   people are scared of us. I like
>   creating but I don't love what I'm
>   writing.

>   JESS
>   It's okay to put it down.

>   LAST CLOWN
>   I wanna love what I'm writing.

>   JESS
>   Well, what is it that you really
>   want to know? Or understand?

>   LAST CLOWN
>   Why do people claim to love
>   children but our foster care system
>   is so broken?

>   JESS
>   Great question. Maybe there's a
>   foster care crusader the world
>   needs to know about? Or a foster
>   kid trying to find his other
>   siblings?

> LAST CLOWN
> I would love to learn more about
> that. But I'm not an expert.

> JESS
> All the better. The story is how
> you share what you learn. You don't
> have to know all the answers. You
> get to find out.

The LAST CLOWN takes off his wig and red nose.

> LAST CLOWN
> But my entire family is clowns.
> Clowns is all I know.

> JESS
> Join the club.

> LAST CLOWN
> I don't have to write what I know?

> JESS
> Please don't. Write what you need
> to learn. And help us all.

The clown sets his nose on the ledge of the tub before
rising. And jingling. He tenderly sets THE KEYS on the ledge

> JESS (CONT'D)
> I've always wanted the keys to the
> clown car. Thanks. You gotta get
> out of here, the readers need an
> outline, a screenplay and some
> never-before-seen scenes with
> cheeky annotations.

Pulling off his clown shoes, the barefoot clown pauses.

> LAST CLOWN
> Hey. What's the Secret Ingredient,
> by the way?

> JESS
> Love.

And with that, the clown nods. Leaving Jess to pop on the red
rubber nose, grab the keys and hold them tightly to her
chest. Closing her eyes and smiling contently as we cut to
BLACK.

PART TWO:

THE BRING IT ON PAGES

THE BRING IT ON PAGES

"Pages" are what screenwriters produce and turn in. It's the term working sceenwriters use.

What follows is a small window into the process of taking a film from idea to full-blown movie.

First: The outline (aka How I Sold It)
Then: The final cut of the movie (aka How You Saw It)
Finally: Annotated/deleted scenes (aka How It Meandered)

I've decided to go with a full quote here for context, 20 years later.

"Within the first two minutes of Bring It On, the film lets us know that it's in on the joke. The Toros' opening cheer is performance art, equal parts self aware and self-criticism. It tells the audience: I know how you might feel about cheerleaders, and frankly, I don't care."

"Rather than simply use the archetypal cheerleader to paint the picturesque high school experience, Bring It On delved deeper into the politics behind the uniforms, telling a story of cultural appropriation long before Hollywood's brazen lack of diversity was part of the mainstream conversation."

"Passing off Bring It On as nothing more than fluffy early-2000s girl-power cinema overlooks the power of the movie's progressive approach to themes of race and class."

IVANA RIHTER
AUG 21, 2000
BUSTLE.COM

Certificate of Registration

This Certificate issued under the seal of the Copyright Office in accordance with title 17, *United States Code*, attests that registration has been made for the work identified below. The information on this certificate has been made a part of the Copyright Office records.

Marybeth Peters

Register of Copyrights, United States of America

Registration Number:

PAu 3-371-583

Effective date of registration:

November 6, 2008

Title

Title of Work: Cheerleading Outline

Contents Titles: Cheerleading Outline

Completion/ Publication

Year of Completion: 1996

Author

■ **Author:** Jessica Bendinger

Author Created: text

Citizen of: United States   **Domiciled in:** United States

Copyright claimant

Copyright Claimant: Jessica Bendinger

███████████████, Los Angeles, CA

Certification

Name: Jessica Bendinger

Date: November 6, 2008

cheerleading outline

1. It's a hot, August afternoon on the intramural field of North Carolina State University. Hundreds of High School girls (and a smattering of guys) crowd the field doing a complicated, drill game of Simon Sez. Welcome to the American Cheerleading Association's National High School Cheerleading camp. Squads from schools all around the country wear their school colors, forming separate color cliques all over the field. Cheerleading Instructors in ACA cheerleading uniforms instruct the campers from raised platforms around the field. Supervisors, school coaches, various sponsor and supply representatives – as well as an impressive array of curious male bystanders – view proceedings from the bleachers. This is another world... with a caste system all its own – complete with all genus of fashion, attitude, and cheerleading ability.

2. **Meet Torrance and Whitney: fun-loving, really good-looking, soon-to-be Seniors and cheerleaders extraordinaire. They've just voted for their new captain, speculating as to who's gonna get the gig. It's girly locker-room talk, and we move from conversation to conversation amongst the various members of their squad: the Filias Deus School Spartans of Santa Ana, California. As they dress, stretch, and adjust their spanky pants, opinions spew forth: 'I did not vote for her!' 'Darcy thinks she should get it cause her dad pays for everything,' 'Jordan'll get it because the guys love lifting her,' 'What about Torrance?' 'Torrance better not get it,' etc. The FDS lay of the land and some inter-personal dynamics of the squad as –**

3. A loud speaker announces: '**Reigning five-time national co-ed champions, the Filias Deus School–** will be performing in 5 minutes. Like a Beatles concert, throngs of campers rush off intramural field and into a gymnasium. The bleachers fill with cheerleaders and anticipation. They're rocking, crying, hyper-ventilating. Sly girlies hide video cameras in teddy bears and pom pons. The PA crackles as the tape is cued. FDS hits the floor. Ten gorgeous girls and ten hot guys stomp, yell and fly through the air at dizzying heights with military precision. Head-banging rock and roll blares through the gymnasium, the perfect accompaniment for the ballistic exhibition performance. FDS rocks, and the vivacious Torrance – head mounter – is clearly the best cheerleader they've got. It's a mixed feeling: at first we think it's ridiculous, but you have to admire the difficulty and the audible-gasp-inducing risk. Their finale: a toss where the tossee catches a gymnasium rafter and hangs for a beat, sends the crowd into eardrum-busting spasms. The campers, supervisors and custodians know they're watching history.

4. **After the performance, departing Captain and bitch-on-wheels, Big Red, makes her twisted retirement speech and announces the new captain, Torrance Shipman.** As Big Red blathers on about her future at Cal State Dominguez Hills, Torrance gets jabbed by a buddy: 'I'd watch that boyfriend of yours...' Torrance's beau will be a sophomore at that very same school. Without warning, the <u>new</u> captain is promptly hazed by her squadmates: tampons, pads and all color and size of condom and condiments get dumped on and attached to her uniform.

5. Last meal at camp: Coach/Advisor Anita Shelton swaps war stories with other supervisors at the mess hall. Blonde, bubbly and chronically hoarse from years of cheerleading ('Friends call me Ni-ni, or Ta-ta'), this mother of two still competes. A 30-something with a penchant for self-aggrandizement, her devotion to the 'Mrs. Cheerleader America' competitions is off-putting. When a fellow advisor expresses dismay diehards want cheerleading considered a sport, Ni-ni shuts the woman right down: "If you think cheerleading isn't a sport, you've missed the game."

6. At other tables, squads from all over the country inter-mingle and gossip. 'Will Memphis Public get a bid to Nationals?' Rumors of a fabulous new California squad simmer. People are saying they're gonna compete and are way ahead of the competition. 'They do it for the thrill of the stunt,' chimes a know-it-all from Nevada. Torrance asks Big Red if any of it is true, and dismissals are Big Red's refrain: 'It's all bull, you hear crap like this every summer. It's just a cheerleading urban legend.' Torrance believes her mentor. **A roll call cheer – that introduces all the male and female members of the FDS squad (complete with candid improvisations) – closes out the dinner... The girls have androgynous names (Courtney, Whitney, Darcy, Carver, Jordan, Danny, Brett), as do the guys (Jan, Leslie, Brook, Kelly, Ronan, Sandy etc.).**

7. **Back home in sunny Santa Ana: Torrance's Mom and Dad – Bruce and Christine Shipman – aren't what you'd expect. A two-career power household, Mom is a part-time lawyer and feminist who'd really like Torrance to expand her interests; Dad's a regional insurance VP who indulges his little girl, but wishes she'd apply to more schools than those with strong cheerleading traditions. Little brother Dustin is an intellectually superior terror who makes merciless fun of big sis. Nice house, nice cars and a daughter who they love... but don't really understand.** The last days of summer before high school rears its ugly head. SAT's, college applications, new hairstyles. Her room is a sanctuary of gymnastics; megaphones; letters and squad paraphernalia. Rumors of a new cute brother and sister transferring into FDS are reaching a feverish pitch.

8. **The Boyfriend. Clear animosity between Torrance's family and Buzz (who doesn't seem to notice they don't like him).** He calls Torrance 'Teetee' and has <u>her</u> packing up <u>his</u> **Geo Tracker as heads back to Cal State Dominguez Hills.** He shows his affection by lifting her into impromptu cheerleading stunts. **One more year and she'll be there, too! A gung-ho cheerleader himself, Buzz's college supplies are oddly devoid of books: garment bags filled with uniforms; megaphones; spirit signs and practice gear. Buzz is a spirit leader extraordinaire, who respects Torrance's devotion to pep.** Their relationship is oddly devoid of sexual chemistry and horny teen behavior.

9. Quick pre-practice meeting establishing frivolity of squad. They're using last year's competition winnings – almost twelve thousand in scholarship money – towards new uniforms, accessories and letter jackets. Looking the best is the key to ESPN glory. The

remaining eight thousand will subsidize competition costs. **Let the practice begin! Intense. A brutal cheerleading boot camp. So intense in fact, the new lead mounter (think top of the pyramid) breaks her leg.** The FDS Dazzlers (the pom pon / dance / drill squad) show up, laughing about the injured member. Bittery, buttery rivalry between two squads...

10. Torrance and Coach Shelton have to get permission from the High School Board and Principal for this year's agenda. And an emergency try-out. Not a popular request, as the school still hasn't settled the lawsuits from parents with kids who didn't make it last year. Too bad. They need a replacement. FDS Dazzler Captain – Pam Ann Jones – in an irritating overture, complains that the cheerleaders get more money than the pom squad. Her request is denied... until the day the Dazzlers win four National Championships in a row.

11. **First day of school!** It's an affluent Catholic/ private school without the uniforms. Fashion improvisation is allowed. Groovy high school stuff. Rock soundtrack blares. Frosh girls blushing and giggling as guys walk down hall. The guys – Brook, Les, Jan and Ronan – turn out to be male cheerleaders in uniform. The regular guys in school ogle Torrance and the cheer chicks. They're all sexy and they all know it. It's cool to be a cheerleader at Filias Deus. The Dazzlers are mocked, but pretty oblivious to it. Dazzler-Cheerleading rivalry is omnipresent. **A fab-looking brother and sister transfer team – The Pantones – stand out. They're from Los Angeles, and they dress to a different, cooler, beat.**

12. **Try Outs! The squad has already chosen who they want – but the new girl, Missy Pantone, shows up. No one knows a thing about her. Missy is an amazing spirit leader and gymnast, with a rebel-vibe: her test is harder than the other girls...** they make her do partner stunts. Missy stops them, insisting she can do a 'death press,' a stunt none of the FDS girls know. **It's undeniably cool. It's obvious she should get on the squad, but the other squad members don't like her, concocting lame excuses. Torrance over-rules the squad, much to their chagrin. Torrance and Missy bond. Other girls resent it.** As they're walking out, a gorgeous guy waits on a moped. Missy says, 'Let me introduce you to **my brother.' Sparks fly. Smells like teen romance for Torrance.**

13. Next day at school: intimidating pep rally where the squad performs. Missy & Cliff are shady with Torrance, brooding about something. At their shared study hall, Missy confronts Torrance. **Missy insists those championship routines are all derivative of the Inglewood Clovers. Who? Torrance is confused, she fought for Missy to get on the squad. Missy thinks it's an act and Torrance is bluffing.**

14. After school, Missy and Cliff are waiting for Torrance in a groovy mobile. **They want to show Torrance a piece of the truth. Bonding and chemistry as they head to...**

15. **A public high-school basketball game. Nothing special, until the Inglewood cheerleading squad hits the floor at half-time. Beyond unbelievable, they are way better than FDS, and even do the hang-from-the-rafters stunt... flawlessly. The crowd – both sides – goes abso-tively ape shit. Our FDS trio stand out in their preppy school garb and get hassled by the Inglewood head cheerleader, Isis (a.k.a. Brandy), "We've seen you on ESPN, doing our shit..." This sassy hip-hop cheer chick proceeds to describe Big Red. 'She's been coming for years, video camera and everything.' Missy is satisfied, Torrance is despondent. Cliff says it's only cheerleading... enough already.**

16. Torrance has seen it, but she doesn't quite believe it. Big Red was her mentor! They worked so hard! She was confident they were the best in the purest way possible. Stricken about what to do, college applications loom large. Big talk with mom and dad about where she's going to go. Tension about Torrance's will vs. parental desire. She'd like Cal State Dom Hills or U. of Memphis or Western Kentucky. Somewhere with a great cheerleading tradition, obviously! Mom and Dad concerned about academic tradition. Where's the future in this hobby? Going pro? 'How bout going to the Olympics? When I win a medal I'm sure you'll say you supported it all along.' They'll entertain Kentucky if she'll entertain UCLA, Berkeley, or mom's alma mater, Pomona. Agreed. Dustin does a cheer about how great she's making him look.

17. Missy's training. Tension on the squad is such that Torrance preps routines with Missy at Missy's house. The Pantones live in a different world. Modern taste and absent parents. Missy and Torr discuss Inglewood situation. They decide not to tell the squad yet. It's too much to learn new routines and unfair to the squad. Two hot guy cheeryL's – Jan & Les – come over to work stunts. They love Missy. While Missy and the boys work outside, Cliff and Torrie have cute moment – he's having a prob with physics and she solves it. He rides her for playing stupid. She rides him for having a pre-conceived notion of a cheerleader IQ. Jan & Les agree to work on the other squad members re. Missy. The core clique is forming.

18. **Torrance trying to reach Buzz. He's super busy, or when she calls – he has roommates tell her he's not there. Shrugs it off. Little bro overhears this speakerphone phone dodging thing and dings her for being a loser-lover.** Says he heard there's a squad that's gonna kick they're ass this year... UCLA, Berkeley, and Pomona applications are staring at her. She starts with Western Kentucky and Memphis...

19. Cliff asks Torrance out at study hall, and she says no because of Buzz. Cliff laughs at her, thinks she's kidding. Considering she says no to him, he really makes her feel like an idiot. **Torrance is attracted to Cliff, and torn.**

8/26/96   cheerleading outline

20. NIGHT GAME! Filias Deus vs. Costa Mesa Catholic. Cars cruising before the game, teens nipping Zima in the bleachers, electricity filling in the air. American Graffiti vibe. Fun! Everything's toasty until Isis and a trio of Inglewood cheerleaders (Jenelope, Trea and Arthurine) show up at the game un-noticed. After the game is underway, the quartet initiate a slow burn. They imitate FDS cheer moves from the stands, eliciting a small bit of attention. Satisfied, they squeeze down into front row and imitate the squad in a bigger way, laughing. Once the FDS girls take notice, the fierce foursome stand in front of FDS squad – face to face – and perform all the cheers by heart, including lifts. FDS Football team sucks and loses. Torrance and Isis face off. The message is loud and clear: Whatever you do, we can do better. Prove it! An out-cheer-each-other-add-on game (Deliverance banjo) commences. Hard to say who's better – both cool, but different. Isis has prepared the last word in a language FDS can understand: a cheer. 'Do our shit, you'll look like shit, cuz we the ones who down with it!'

21. Torrance starts realizing they may not be the best, and is devastated. She has to be the best, and calls Buzz for advice. He puts her off. Torrance is frantic, "I don't know what to do here, this is serious!" Totally distracted and disinterested, Buzz lam~ly tries to calm her, telling if she won't cheat and use stolen material, she'll have to do what the other nationally ranked squads do... hire someone. It's not totally legal, but the ACA never finds out. Funny disillusionment meltdown for Torrie as Buzz tells her about all these legendary squads she's worshipped having done it. 'Everybody does it. Everybody cheats,' he says, 'Call this guy. He worked with University of Memphis... ' 'U of Memphis?' Torrance enthuses, dazzled by the thought.

22. On the phone with choreographer Sparky from Chattanooga. Hard-core, tough negotiation exchange. Missy steps in and hard-balls him. One week looks like one thousand dollars plus airfare. They go to Darcy's daddy – she says no. Winter Formal fundraiser is too far away. Cut to: Very arch homage to the Bikini car wash. The girls are causing accidents. The guys in speedos causing accidents. Cars lined up for blocks. Guy cheerleaders working the Olympic swimming look, looking buff. Torrance calls Buzz to come help, he can't do it. Missy tells Torrie to call Cliff – he'll do it. Ten teams of two, sudsing and spraying. – It's very sexy, very over the top. Gets even sexier when Cliff shows up to help. When he pulls off his shirt, Torrance loses herself for a minute. This is not lost on Cliff. At $10/a car, the carwash pulls in about $1500.

23. Airport pick up. **Sparky arrives.** Stays with the Pantones. Torrance, Missy, Jan and Les go over the week's agenda. **Sparky is a total slave driver**: a Just-Out-Of-College, Cheer-frenzied go-getter. Sparky demos routine in Pantone living room to Torrance, Missy, Jan and Les. **Very 'white guy trying to be funky.' The music is a very white hip-hop mix. Way behind the curve, Sparky is a little off, a little too into it.**

24. Torrance relieved to have someone else taking over. Coach Shelton not only is thrilled with the new blood, but is flirting shamelessly with him. Sparky wants them to do **a really hard move: the wolf's wall.** Torrance and Missy, Jan & Les think they can do it. Rest of the squad is chicken. Can't quite get it now, but maybe by Nationals. They're using mini-tramps and weird banner signs to accentuate t**he routine. Pretty corny, but it's too late to turn back.** Dazzlers bitching about all the gym time, the cheeryL's have to keep it a secret so Pam Ann won't blow the whistle. They get Jan to distract Pam Ann by pretending he likes her. Mean.

25. Fed up with not reaching Buzz, Torrance drives up to CSDH. En route to his dorm, she catches him making out with Big Red. They don't see her. She watches from afar, devastated. She drives home alone, trying not to cry, and crying harder as a result.

26. Cliff asks what's wrong. Torrance confides. Cliff is not exactly sympathetic, 'What do you expect? He was a cheerleader!!' 'If you hate cheering so much why did you want to go out with me?' 'I didn't realize you'd convinced yourself that's all you are.' Torrance wants to go for it with Cliff. Cliff doesn't like the idea of a rebound and tells her to back off. Just what Torrance needs before...

27. REGIONALS at Magic Mountain! Big crowds, tons of schools competing, very big day. Thumping music and hundreds of cheer and dance squad members sweating for one of three bids to Nationals. FDS are pretty much a lock. Waiting to go on, FDS sees another squad carrying mini-tramps and banners. No biggie, coincidence. It's Tustin, they don't have the stunts. **Inglewood performs early, unveiling a wild, new routine. Fabulous.** Isis wishes Torrance good luck and apologizes for being harsh. Nice moment. **FDS hears their music as they wait backstage. Coincidence? They perform. The crowd seems uncomfortable. The FDS squad work their asses off, but practically get booed. As they exit, an ACA official pulls Torrance and Coach Shelton aside. A third squad has already complained to the board. They suspect choreography! Torrance and Coach reprimanded. They could be disqualified, moment of doubt as to whether they'll get a bid to Nationals. Big Red and Buzz (competing in collegiate division) ride Torrance for wrecking FDS tradition. She rides them for being lying cowards. ACA judges decide to give FDS a bid as they are reigning champions, but they are banned from doing the offending routine.**

28. **Missy calls Tor – great news! Inglewood not sure they can afford to go to Nationals at $400 per girl... isn't that great? Torrance goes mental. Meltdown. 'After all this, and they're not going? They better f-ing perform, or I'll go insane!'**

29. **Torrance asks her dad if he can get anyone in his Inglewood division to sponsor the Clovers. She's determined that they perform – if she's going to win, she wants compete against the best.** Mom is bugging about college applications. Dustin is bugging, period. Family tension. Dad says he'll look into it. Drive to distraction by this

twist, Torrance calls: the ACA; ESPN; commercial sponsors of the NHCC; KTLA; and the LA Times and tells them about Inglewood's plight. Her parents think it's sweet. Little do they know it's <u>also</u> motivated by her insane cheerleading competitive streak.

30. Meet the Clovers Eccentric Chaperone (drag queen, dubious character / older sibling who wants trip to Florida) Patti LaBelle / RuPaul cameo. A diva who rehearses the Inglewood squad into the ground. Personalities of Inglewood squad emerging, celebrating donations for their trip to Florida, and coveting first prize. **Fierce world of awesome confidence and attitude. The chicks are cool, and they could really use the scholarship money.**

31. **FDS squad breaking into cliques and wars. They can't find a groove, and are pissed at Torrance for fucking with a system that's worked for 4 years. Torrance is freaking: she has cheerleading block. Missy, Jan and Les help her do research: MGM Musicals; MTV videos; Pilobolus and obscure dance troupes; 'Can't Stop the Music'; 'Xanadu'; practicing 'The Wolf's Wall.' Everyone's still a little scared to do it – except Torrance. The foursome re-build the routine and start piecing it together. Teamwork.**

32. Torrance makes another play for Cliff, inviting him to the Winter Formal. Flirty and cool, it is the cheeryL's big fund-raiser for the year... and she's influenced it in a way that reveals Cliff's effect on her taste. Cliff rejects Torrance as shallow, incapable of thinking on her own. She throws it right back at him – he doesn't know what he's talking about, he's not even giving her a chance. Cliff tells her she's going to end up like Coach Shelton if she's not careful.

33. Winter Formal! TURF SCANDAL. Pam Ann has coerced some FDS guys to bring Isis, Trea and Arthurine as escorts. The ultimate Dazzler dis, Missy, Torrie, Jan and Les are shocked. Cheer catfight with Dazzler squad. Pam Ann accuses Torrance of being a racist. Torrance looks Isis straight in the eye and responds: "This isn't about color, this is about school colors. This is about cheerleading." Fun dance scene. Cliff shows up for a dance with Torrance, conceding that he's been the shallow one...

34. FDS leaves for **Nationals** @ Sea World. **Squads in matching travel outfits at airport. Major ESPN hoopla. Registration. Free gift packs. Major corporate dough. Media coverage. The sponsors love the mix this year.** Diva Inglewood chaperone reads Coach Shelton and reduces her to tears.

35. **Inglewood unveils their routine. The earth moves.** FDS huddle before they go on: Torrance insists they go for the Wolf's Wall – squad insists they don't need it. Torrance insists if they're going to win... it has to be because they're the best. **FDS unveils their new routine. It's amazing and totally fresh**, and Torrance nails the landing, but hurts herself.

8/26/96   cheerleading outline

36. **Standing in the ESPN winner's circle are the Inglewood Clovers, holding a giant check for $20,000. FDS stands off to one side, Runner's Up.** The Emcee announces the award they've all been waiting for: Cheerleader of the Year. The Emcee reveals Inglewood anecdote: "For her tireless sportsmanship and selfless efforts in helping squads besides her own, the winner is: Torrance Shipman."

37. Torrance loads college textbooks into a UCLA knapsack, and heads into a lecture hall, followed by... Cliff. He steals a pen out of the pocket of her book bag and kisses her sweetly. They are clearly a couple, and clearly in love. He pulls a letter from Missy out of his pocket, and they take turns reading aloud. Humorous updates on all the poop back home, and how badly the squad sucks without Torrance. Tor mumbles something cryptic that suggests she's thrilled she's no longer in the high school cheerleading game...

38. Coda: Big Red and Buzz are about two years older, and in a pissy mood watching ESPN. As we zoom into the tv screen, a college football half-time show in in progress. A collegiate cheerleading squad dazzles. A familiar face is full screen: It's Torrance. Smiling, yelling, cheering with a vengeance on national television. We pull out to reveal that Torrance is lead mounter on the UCLA squad, cheering next to...none other than Isis.

39. In voice-over, we hear Torrance's voice: "Dear International Olympic Committee, I'm writing hoping you'll consider a new sport for the exhibition spot at the next Olympics..."

BRING IT ON

Written by

Jessica Bendinger

AUGUST 25, 2000
FINAL CUT

INT. HIGH SCHOOL GYMNASIUM

A CO-ED HIGH-SCHOOL CHEERLEADING SQUAD performs center-court.

Like an ESTHER WILLIAMS/MICKEY MOUSE CLUB sequence the SQUAD MOVES and CHEERS in unison.

BIG RED, a sexy, 18-year old with red ringlets and a black heart, commands the floor. RCH in chenille, s-t-r-e-t-c-h-e-s across her sweater.

>   BIG RED
>   (4/4 time, chanting)
>   I'm sexy. I'm cute. I'm popular to
>   boot.

>   SQUAD MEMBERS
>   (4/4 time, joining)
>   I'm bitchin', great hair. The boys
>   all love to stare. I'm wanted, I'm
>   hot I'm everything you're not. I'm
>   pretty, I'm cool, I dominate this
>   school. Who am I? Just guess. Guys
>   wanna touch my chest. I'm rockin'.
>   I smile. And many think I'm vile.
>   I'm flyin'. I jump. You can look
>   but don't you hump. I'm major. I
>   roar. I swear I'm not a whore! We
>   cheer and we lead. We act like
>   we're on speed. Hate us 'cause
>   we're beautiful? Well, we don't
>   like you either! We're
>   cheerleaders. We are cheerleaders!

EACH FEMALE CHEERLEADER springs into frame via JUMP or STUNT.

>   BIG RED
>   Call me Big Red!

WHITNEY DOW, 16, is tan, tan, tan.

>   WHITNEY
>   I'm Wh-Wh-Whitney.

Icy Breck-Girl blonde, COURTNEY EGGBERT, 16, flips between bitchy passivity and bitchy impertinence. Nightmare.

>   COURTNEY
>   Cu-Cu-Cu-Courtney!

Jet-black Lulu bob and movie-star attitude, DARCY ESTRADA is a rich, 17-year-old know-it-all. Stacked.

                    DARCY
          Dude, it's Darcy!

Hello, horsey girl. CARVER RIZCHEK is a 16-year-old rep for
Thighs-R-US.

                    CARVER
          I'm Big Bad Carver, yeah!

15-year-old KASEY is a scrawny mess, whose braces are about
to blind you.

                    KASEY
          Just call me Kasey.

Big Red takes up center position again.

                    BIG RED
          I'm still Big Red.

ENTIRE SQUAD STOPS in their tracks and collectively points
toward Big Red.

                    BIG RED (CONT'D)
               (in 4/4 time)
          I sizzle, I scorch / But now I pass
          the torch / The ballots are in /
          and one girl had to win / She's
          perky, she's fun, and now she's
          number one / K-K-Kick it, Torrance.
          T-T-T-Torrance!

BIRDS EYE VIEW. POM PONS cover the screen, and TORRANCE
SHIPMAN, a vivacious, blonde 17-year-old, smiles broadly as
the poms part ways.

                    TORRANCE
          I'm strong and I'm loud / I'm gonna
          make you proud / I'm T-T-T-
          Torrance. Your captain Torrance.

                    SQUAD
          Let's go, Toros.

                    SQUAD
          We are the Toros / The mighty,
          mighty Toros / We're so terrific,
          we must be Toros! Yea! Go, Toros!
          Yea, come on! Toros!

                    STUDENT BODY CROWD
          - Yeah! All right! - Go, Toros!

3.

Finishing the chant, the girls move into pre-toe-touch-jump position. Torrance smiles broadly before lift-off. Pushing off the floor in slow motion...

The STUDENT BODY CROWD gasps collectively, some MALE CROWD MEMBERS smiling and high-fiving each other.

                    STUDENT BODY CROWD (CONT'D)
          Oh, my God / Nice rack/ Oh, baby --

Torrance's face morphs from glee to panic, her mouth becoming a SCREAM. The camera ZOOMS into Torrance's UVULA, her SCREAMING mixing with the sound of an ALARM CLOCK brrringing as we...cut to

INT. TORRANCE'S ROOM - MORNING

Torrance bolting upright in bed, still SCREAMING bloody murder.

                    TORRANCE
          Holy shit.

TITLES: BRING IT ON

EXT. SHIPMAN HOUSE - DAY

Honking is AARON GILBERT, 18, a great-looking dude: Tan, muscular and not a hair out of place. He pulls curbside in his Geo Tracker, loaded down with guy crap for college.

BRUCE and CHRISTINE SHIPMAN, mid 40's and attractive, are carrying stacks of legal files to their Escort Wagon.

                    AARON
          Hey, hey, Mr. and Mrs. "S."

                    MR. SHIPMAN
               (nausea)
          Oh, look, it's Aaron.

                    MRS. SHIPMAN
               (headachy)
          Oh. Hello, Aaron.

                    AARON
          Hey, can I help?

                    MRS. SHIPMAN
          Oh, no. We're fine, thanks. Really.
          Stay in your vehicle.

                         AARON
          Nuh, nuh, nuh. You sure?

Torrance bounds out of the front door, carrying practice
gear. She kisses her dad en route to Aaron's truck.

                         TORRANCE
          Bye! Be back later!

                    MR. & MRS. SHIPMAN
               (jointly queasy)
          Bye, honey.

INT. AARON'S TRACKER - CONTINUOUS

Torrance leaps into the truck and leans over to kiss Aaron.
Aaron pulls back, uncomfortable.

                         AARON
          Come on, Tor. Can't mack on you in
          front of the parentals.

We hold on Torrance's face, confused by the dust-off. Aaron,
oblivious, throws the Tracker into gear --

                    AARON (CONT'D)
               (to the Shipmans)
          Bye-bye!

EXT. SHIPMAN HOUSE - CONTINUOUS

-- burning a little rubber in the process. The Shipmans wave.

                    MRS. SHIPMAN
          Remember, he's leaving for college.

                    MR. SHIPMAN
          Right.

EXT. NEIGHBORHOOD - DAY

                    TORRANCE
          So, are you excited?

INT. AARON'S TRACKER - DAY

                    AARON
          Oh, yeah! It's college, Tor. I'm
          really stoked, you know? It's just,
          you know, I'm gonna miss you.

5.

                         TORRANCE
               Really?

                         AARON
               Yeah. But next year, it'll be you
               and me reunited at Cal State
               Dominguez Hills. I'll be the
               experienced sophomore; you'll be
               the hot, new freshman.

Torrance tries her best to smile at that thought.

                         AARON (CONT'D)
               Yup. It'll be just like high
               school, only better. Dorm rooms.

                         TORRANCE
               Hmm.

EXT. RANCHO CARNE HIGH SCHOOL - DAY

Aaron glides the Tracker into a space.

                         AARON
               I got the door, Tor.

                         TORRANCE
               Okay.

                         AARON
                    (cheering)
               I got the door, Tor.

Aaron opens the door for Torrance.

                         STUDENT #1
               What's up, Aaron?

                         AARON
               Hey, what up...?

Aaron high-fives a couple people.

                         AARON (CONT'D)
                    (turning to Torrance)
               Hey, hey, remember, when you get
               captain, act surprised, okay?

                         TORRANCE
               Don't jinx me.

Courtney and Whitney approach.

>   WHITNEY
>   Hi, Torrance.

>   COURTNEY
>   Hey, Aaron.

>   AARON
>   Ah, ladies.

>   COURTNEY
>   Good luck at school.

>   AARON
>   Thank you.

>   WHITNEY
>   Oh, Aaron, come to one last
>   practice? You know you're still my
>   favorite cheerleader.

>   AARON
>   Aww.

>   WHITNEY
>   Please?

>   AARON
>   Oh, I'm sorry, guys. I gotta run.

Torrance looks at Aaron, disappointed.

>   TORRANCE
>   You're not staying for the vote?

>   AARON
>   I really gotta beat traffic. I
>   can't be late for orientation.

>   TORRANCE
>   But I really want...

Before she can say more, he kisses her on the lips. A long,
hot kiss.

>   AARON
>   Mmm. Trust me. You're gonna get it.

He gives her a big sexy smile. Torrance musters a smile of
her own, then nods understandingly.

>   AARON (CONT'D)
>   Buh-bye.

77

7.

                    TORRANCE
          Bye.

INT. LOCKER ROOM - DAY

Girls are in various states of undress. Our main girls
(Whitney, Courtney, Darcy, Carver, and Kasey) are getting
dressed for practice. Speculation fills the air.

                    WHITNEY
          Did you vote?

                    COURTNEY
          Oh, yeah. Darcy thinks she should
          get captain 'cause her dad pays for
          everything.

                    WHITNEY
          He should use some of that money to
          buy her a clue.

IN ANOTHER PART OF THE LOCKER ROOM

                    KASEY
          Courtney'll get captain. The guys
          love clutching her butt.

                    DARCY
          Yeah, she's got a lot to hang on
          to. What's plural for "butt"? On
          one person, I mean.

                    CARVER
          She puts the "ass" in "massive."

Darcy checks out Carver's sizeable rear end.

                    DARCY
          You put the "lude" in "deluded."

Big Red appears, and makes her way to the girls.

                    BIG RED
          Yo! Can I have all your votes?

                    CARVER
          Mine.

                    DARCY
          Here's me.

                    BIG RED
          Thank you.

The girls hand their slips to Big Red who ambles. The squad
rolls their eyes collectively.

>   TORRANCE
>   We should get Big Red a gift, or at
>   least someone should say something.

Courtney and Whitney exchange loaded glances.

>   COURTNEY
>   Pass.

>   WHITNEY
>   Good riddance. I don't believe in
>   ass-mosis.

>   TORRANCE
>   It's not brown-nosing. She's the
>   departing captain. She did a lot
>   for this squad. Oh, come on. Both
>   of you sucked before she whipped
>   you into shape.

>   COURTNEY
>   Oh, whipped? Is that what that was?

>   WHITNEY
>   No one will miss Big Red, Tor. She
>   puts the "itch" in "bitch. "

>   COURTNEY
>   She puts the "whore " in
>   "horrifying."

>   TORRANCE
>   You know, it's her last practice.
>   How would you feel?

>   COURTNEY
>   Big Red has no feelings.

>   WHITNEY
>   Just testicles.

EXT. FOOTBALL FIELD - DAY

Big Red stands in front of the impatient squad, all
anticipating who will be named captain.

>   BIG RED
>   You guys are all great athletes.
>   Thanks in large part to me.
>   (MORE)

> BIG RED (CONT'D)
> And I know that your new captain
> will keep the tradition alive,
> leading you to the record sixth
> national cheerleading championship
> you know is yours.

Torrance is flanked by LES and JAN, two male cheerleaders,
who she squeezes for support.

> BIG RED (CONT'D)
> So, let's meet your new leader,
> Torrance Shipman.

The squad members whoop and shout.

> TORRANCE
> Oh, my God!

Torrance, Les, and Jan all leap up and hug. Courtney and
Whitney roll their eyes and give each other "I told ya so"
looks.

> COURTNEY
> That slut.

> TORRANCE
> Okay, listen up! I'd like to try a
> wolf wall.

The rest of the squad erupts into LAUGHTER.

> CARVER
> Oh, excellent!

Courtney seizes the opportunity and puts a palm on Torrance's
forehead.

> COURTNEY
> Torrance has got the fever, people.

> KASEY
> What's a wolf's wall?

> JAN
> Only the hardest pyramid known to
> cheerleading. And mankind.

> DARCY
> The words "big" and "britches" come
> to mind.

> WHITNEY
> She's crazy. She'll kill us all.

> COURTNEY
> Hello! Some of us have not spent
> the entire summer working out.
> Right, Carver?

Carver scoffs.

> TORRANCE
> Come on, guys! Let's be different
> for once. We can't just rest on our
> laurels.

> JAN
> Why does everybody say that? Maybe
> a laurel's a good place to rest.

For all their joking, it's obvious most of the squad is
scared shitless. Then...

> LES
> Come on, man. You guys suck. Let's
> do this.

Les leaps up to join Torrance as the rest of the squad
GRUMBLES in agreement.

They take up positions and try the "build".

> TORRANCE
> One, two, three, four, five, six,
> seven, eight-

It crumbles. A second time.

> TORRANCE (CONT'D)
> Five, six, seven, eight. Kick one-

It falls. A third time, they almost nail it.

> TORRANCE (CONT'D)
> Five, six, seven, eight. And one!
> Stick it! Come on, girls! Stick it
> for me!

Fourth time...they try again.

> TORRANCE (CONT'D)
> Five, six, seven, eight. Go one,
> two, three, four, five, six, seven,
> eight. Kick one! Good job! Whoo!

They STICK it. Carver perches at the very top.

                         LES
              Pinch some pennies. Someone's
              slackin'.

                         JAN
              Do I look like a milk maid? 'Cause
              somebody feels like a cow!

                         TORRANCE
              Carver, can you cradle out?

                         CARVER
              You bet I can.

CARVER'S POV: from atop the pyramid. Looking down, three body
lengths high, we feel the vertigo. It's high.

                         TORRANCE
              Okay, ready? One, two, down, up!

Carver attempts it, but she's off-balance.

                         SQUAD
              Carver? Carver!

EXT. AMBULANCE/FOOTBALL FIELD - DAY

Carver lies on the ground, already in a neck brace. Pull out
to show an ambulance and EMERGENCY MEDICAL TECHNICIANS
loading Carver, on a stretcher- into the vehicle. Our eight
lead kids look on, distraught.

                         TORRANCE
              Carver, are you okay?

                         CARVER
              I'm fine, really. Don't you guys
              worry about me. It's just a
              scratch. I'll be back to practice
              tomorrow, so don't you guys fret,
              okay? And I don't want you to worry
              at all, because I'm a quick healer.
              I promise, you guys. I'm gonna be
              there for you. You hear me? Guys?
              Bye!

Torrance looks especially upset. Behind her, Courtney and
Whitney shake their heads.

INT. SHIPMAN KITCHEN - THAT NIGHT

Bummed out, Torrance trudges into the kitchen where her mom
sits at the table. Seated beside her is little bother JUSTIN,
14. He acts like he smells: bad.

> TORRANCE
> I got captain.

> JUSTIN
> Yeah, and you sent a girl to the
> hospital on your first day. Aye,
> aye, Captain!

> TORRANCE
> You were listening on the phone?
> Mom!

> JUSTIN
> It's true. She really should get
> her own private line, you know.
> She's growing up so fast.

> MRS. SHIPMAN
> Justin, go away.

> JUSTIN
> At ease, Captain.

> TORRANCE
> Oh, shut up.

He exits, and Mrs. Shipman picks up an envelope and an
official-looking paper: Torrance's class schedule.

> MRS. SHIPMAN
> Well, this blistering academic
> schedule shouldn't get in your way.
> You should be happy about that.

> TORRANCE
> Why can't you accept the fact that
> I'm not a genius? It just kills you
> that I'm not an honor student.

> MRS. SHIPMAN
> No. It kills me that you barely
> make time to study. If you studied
> half as much as you cheer, you'd be
> in great shape. Your priorities are-

> TORRANCE
> No! Those are your priorities! Mine
> are just fine.

13.

                         MRS. SHIPMAN
              Look, I'm just saying that college
              might be less of a shock if you
              take an extra lab or language
              course or something. What do you
              think?

                         TORRANCE
              Will Advanced Chem get you off my
              back?

                         MRS. SHIPMAN
              Not completely, but it'll help.

                         TORRANCE
              Done. You know, mothers have killed
              to get their daughters on squads.

                         MRS. SHIPMAN
              That mother didn't kill anyone. She
              hired a hit man.

INT. CLASSROOM - DAY ADDED SCENE

CLIFF, a hunky, 17-year-old, glides into the room in a well-
preserved CLASH T-Shirt, and complete with a walk-man
headset. From the reactions of the crowd, he's a new
commodity. Dressed differently from the rest of the kids.

                         TEACHER
              Everyone, we have a new student
              transferring from Mission Hills
              High School in Los Angeles. Please
              welcome Cliff "Pant One."

                         CLIFF
                    (correcting her
                     pronunciation)
              Pantone. Thanks.

Cliff goes to take the only open seat, right next to
Torrance. He walks past two male students, RCH QUARTERBACK
and RCH TIGHT END, who are already poking fun.

                         RCH QUARTERBACK
                    (sneezes)
              Loser!

The RCH Tight End laughs.

                         RCH QUARTERBACK (CONT'D)
                    (sneezes)
              Loser!

                    CLIFF
          Wait, wait, wait. Was that, uh- Was
          that the "loser sneeze" I just
          heard right there? Guys, come on. I
          mean, what is that, from like the
          1900s? Nobody does that anymore. I
          don't think anybody does. When I
          lived in Kentucky... Did they still
          do the loser sneeze in Kentucky?

He pauses and rubs his chin while pondering.

                    CLIFF (CONT'D)
          No. They had, uh, guns and homemade
          bombs. What about L.A.? There was a
          lot of attitude in L.A., but no
          loser sneeze. I'm pretty sure the
          loser sneeze is officially dead.
          Sorry.

                    RCH QUARTERBACK
               (sneezing again)
          Loser!

The two bullies high-five.

                    RCH TIGHT END
          Nice.

                    TORRANCE
          I don't think they got the memo
          about the loser sneeze.

Cliff turns to see Torrance, surprised that she is talking to
him, and instantly smitten.

                    CLIFF
          Uh, no, apparently not. Cliff.

                    TORRANCE
          Torrance.

Torrance is completely flummoxed from the chemistry. Noticing
the large book on her desk-

                    CLIFF
          Advanced Chem. Yikes.

                    TORRANCE
          Um, 'fraid so. Are you intimidated?

                    CLIFF
          Y-Yeah, a little.

                    TORRANCE
          Really?

                    CLIFF
     No, not really.

                    TORRANCE
               (referencing his t-shirt)
          So, is that your band or something?

                    CLIFF
     The Clash? No, uh- It's a British
     punk band, circa 1977 to 1983-ish.
     Original lineup, anyway.

                    TORRANCE
          How vintage.

The bell rings, and they pack up their books.

                    CLIFF
     Um, so I'll see you around then?

                    TORRANCE
          Looks like it.

EXT. RANCHO CARNE HIGH - DAY

The RCH Quarterback and Tight End walk by Les and Jan.

                    RCH QUARTERBACK
          Hey, hey, hey, hey. Whoa! It's sexy
          Leslie and Jan, Jan, the
          cheerleading man.

                    RCH TIGHT END
          Hey, fags.

Jan, clearly sick of this rill, rises to confront them, but
Les holds him back.

                    LES
          Whoa, whoa. Just because we won
          more trophies than you guys, that's
          no reason to go get all malignant.

                    RCH TIGHT END
          Malignant this, tool.

The PLAYERS grin stupidly, laughing as they head into school.

                    RCH QUARTERBACK
          Nice!

Jan grits his teeth, pissed.

                    JAN
          One of these days, man.

                    LES
          Let it go. They never even won a
          single game. Gotta be kind of rough
          on 'em. Besides, they're dicks.

                    JAN
          Yeah, yeah, yeah.

                    TORRANCE
          Les, tell me you have Advanced Chem
          first period.

                    LES
          Advanced Chem, first period.

                    TORRANCE
          If you have a lab partner already,
          I'm screwed.

                    LES
          Torrance, it's only the second day
          of school, and your academic
          insecurity bit is completely tired.
          You know, everyone's saying your
          ambition broke Carver's leg.

                    TORRANCE
          When, really, it was the angle at
          which she slammed into the ground.

                    LES
          Kasey did a massive e-mail last
          night. Misspelled "leg."

                    TORRANCE
          Shut up!

                    LES
          Two G's. Apparently, Carver gets
          home schooling for the next three
          months.

                    TORRANCE
          I'm cursed. Replacing her is gonna
          be a nightmare.

                    LES
          Well, that's why you're the
          captain, Captain.

INT. GYMNASIUM - DAY

The squad huddles before try-outs.

                    DARCY
          Bring on the tyros, the neophytes
          and the dilettanti.

                    JAN
          SAT's are over, Darcy.

                    DARCY
               (to Jan)
          And you're still jealous of my
          score.
               (to squad)
          Are we sure Carver's not
          malingering?

                    TORRANCE
          Carver will strictly be cheering in
          Special Olympics until March.
          Nationals are February 10th.
          Regionals are in, like, four weeks.
          I talked to her. She's cool with
          this.

                    COURTNEY
          Don't tell me Carver can cut school
          just because she broke her leg in
          three places. Hello! Get a
          wheelchair!

                    WHITNEY
          That lucky bitch.

                    COURTNEY
               (to Torrance)
          Tell me we're not actually
          continuing this masquerade and
          having tryouts. Let's cut the crap
          and pick somebody now. Whitney's
          little sister Jamie is really
          teeny. She'll be easy to toss, and
          she doesn't give lip.

                    JAN
          Just tongue.

                    WHITNEY
          Kiss my ass, Jan.

                    JAN
          I'd love to.

                    TORRANCE
          If she's the best, Jamie's got it.
          But we have to see everyone.

MOANS from squad.

INT. GYMNASIUM - CONTINUOUS

TRYOUT MONTAGE

Quick cuts AUDITIONERS going through paces:

-START-OVER GIRL, confused, tries to get through her cheer

                    START-OVER GIRL
          Ready, okay. Wait. Hold on. Let me
          try that again. That was terrible.
                (pausing, readying)
          Ready, okay! Go, team... Ready,
          okay! Sorry.
                (she attempts again)
          Ready, okay! Shit.

ON THE SQUAD, trying to stay upbeat and focused.

-BE AGGRESSIVE GIRL, zero energy.

                    BE AGGRESSIVE GIRL
          Be aggressive. Be, be aggressive.

-ARGUMENTATIVE GIRL has a few questions before beginning.

                    ARGUMENTATIVE GIRL
          How many cheers do we have to
          memorize? Do we get paid for this?
          And do I have to provide my own
          uniform?

-DANCING GUY. A glasses and braces-wearing KID launches into
the "Robot"

-Argumentative Girl, again

                    ARGUMENTATIVE GIRL (CONT'D)
          And I see you guys are wearing red.
          Um, that just does not work for me.

-BEEN-CRYING-FOR-HOURS GIRL tries to smiles through red,
puffy eyes and a devastated disposition.

                    BEEN-CRYING-FOR-HOURS-GIRL
          Ready, okay! R-C-H! Toros all the
          way!

19.

ON KASEY: Tearing up out of sympathy

>   BEEN-CRYING-FOR-HOURS-GIRL (CONT'D)
>   (breaks down into sobs)
>   I'm sorry. I just broke up with my
>   boyfriend.

-BALLET BOY graciously moving through his moment like he's in tights and Swan Lake.

>   LES
>   (impressed)
>   Pretty good.

-PREPPY GIRL steps up awkwardly. She's the WHITEST girl you've ever seen -- until she opens her mouth. She starts moving wildly and speaking in an unexpected Brooklyn accent.

>   PREPPY GIRL
>   Yo, yo, yo! What's up? What's up?
>   It's time to get busy! So let's
>   kick this shit and rock the C. K.
>   off your panties, yeah.

CUT TO TORRANCE AND THE SQUAD, horrified.

-THEATRE BOY wears a mock turtle neck and black jeans. He's singing his heart out and gesticulating grandly.

>   THEATRE BOY
>   Give my regards to Broadway!
>   Remember me to Herald Square. Tell
>   all the gang-

>   COURTNEY
>   Excuse me! What's with the song?

>   THEATRE BOY
>   Isn't this the audition for Pippin?

>   COURTNEY
>   No.

- STRIPPER CHEERLEADER, mortifying our squad with inappropriately salacious dance moves. As she climbs on the table, Jan is knocked out of his chair.

>   JAN
>   (recovering)
>   Okay, uh, any more questions? I
>   think we're good.

- JAMIE, Whitney's sister and a ridiculously tiny freshman, steps up next.

                    WHITNEY
          Here's our girl.

Jamie breezes through her try-out unspectacularly, knowing
she's a shoo-in.

                    JAMIE
          Rancho Carne's not all talk / All
          we know is Toros rock. / Shake your
          booties, Scream and shout / Toro
          players work it out. Go, Toros.

Jamie finishes up clumsily, then WINKS at the squad. Torrance
turns to Whitney and Courtney, raising an eyebrow.

                    ARGUMENTATIVE GIRL
          Do I have to wear those little
          underwear things? 'Cause I don't
          like wearing underwear.

                    TORRANCE
          Thanks!

Just as they think they are done, the door opens again. A
STRAGGLER walks in. Brunette 16-year-old wearing low-slung
cholo trousers. Baroque black tattoos ring around one bicep.

                    WHITNEY
          Excuse me. Where'd you park your
          Harley? Get real.

MISSY PANTONE looks more like a roadie for Social Distortion
than a cheerleading candidate. Jan checks her out.

                    COURTNEY
          Tattoos are strictly verboten.
          Sorry.

Missy licks her middle finger thoroughly, and just when you
think she's going to flip the bird, she runs it over the
tattoo, smearing it.

                    MISSY
          Sorry. I got bored during fourth
          period.

                    WHITNEY
          You need to fill one of these out.

                    MISSY
               (producing form)
          Did it.

91

> DARCY
> (looking at form)
> Missy, is it? Okay, before we
> start, I'm afraid we're gonna need
> to make sure you can do a standing
> back tuck. Standard procedure. You
> understand.

Missy drops her chain-key-chain to the floor with a CLUNK.

> MISSY
> Standing back handspring back tuck
> okay?

Missy quickly executes a standing back handspring back tuck
layout. It's Miller time. Shannon Miller. Jan is especially
impressed.

> WHITNEY
> Where's this girl from, Romania?

> COURTNEY
> Can she yell?

> TORRANCE
> We'll try an oldie. Awesome, oh,
> wow! Like, totally freak me out! I
> mean, right on! The Toros sure are
> number one.

> MISSY
> (screaming, cheer-like)
> I transferred from Los Angeles!
> Your school has no gymnastics team!
> This is a last resort!
> Okay, so I've never cheered before.
> So what? How about something that
> actually requires neurons?

> COURTNEY
> (to Whitney)
> Do it.

> WHITNEY
> Front handspring, step out, round
> off, back handspring, step out,
> round off, back hand spring, full
> twisting lay out.

Missy performs this perfectly.

> SQUAD
> Ha! - Hey!

> TORRANCE
> (to squad)
> Missy is bank.

> COURTNEY
> Uh, bankrupt. We've already so
> decided on Jamie.

> TORRANCE
> Courtney, this is not a democracy.
> It's a "cheerocracy." I'm sorry,
> but I'm overruling you.

> COURTNEY
> You are being a "cheertator,"
> Torrance, and a pain in my ass! We
> already voted. Besides, Missy looks
> like an uber dyke.

This is not lost on Missy. A door SLAMS, Missy's gone.

> TORRANCE
> Courtney, I'm the captain. I'm
> pulling rank, and you can fall in
> line or not. If we're gonna be the
> best, we have to have the best.
> Missy's the poo. So take a big
> whiff.

EXT. PANTONE HOUSE - DAY

Torrance rings a DOORBELL. The door opens, changing her
demeanor noticeably. Hard to tell why until we see...

Cliff from English class. Foreigner T-shirt, baggy chinos and
short spiky hair. He looks as surprised as Torrance. They
snatch mutual stares.

> CLIFF
> You.

> TORRANCE
> And you.
> (recovering)
> I mean, hi. I'm..

> CLIFF
> (surprised)
> A cheerleader.

Torrance looks down at her uniform, then back to Cliff.

                    TORRANCE
          Uh, yeah. Head cheerleader, to be
          exact.

                    CLIFF
          Wow.

                    TORRANCE
          So does Missy live here?

                    CLIFF
          Uh, actually, she moved back to
          L.A., yeah. Something about evil
          cheerleaders or-

                    TORRANCE
          Look, I'm serious. We have to get
          her.

                    CLIFF
          Is her drug dependency gonna be a
          problem?

Missy appears at the door.

                    MISSY
               (to Cliff)
          Cliff, shut up.
               (to Torrance)
          What do you want?

                    TORRANCE
          I want you on the squad. You're the
          best. They know it. They just
          reject the unfamiliar.

                    MISSY
          Thanks, but no, thanks. I mean, I
          plead temporary insanity. See, I'm
          a hard-core gymnast. No way jumping
          up and down, screaming, "Go, team,
          go!" is gonna satisfy me.

                    TORRANCE
          Look, we're gymnasts, too, except
          no beam, no bars, no vault.

                    MISSY
          Sorry. Not interested.

Missy goes to close the door, but Cliff stops her.

                  MISSY (CONT'D)
           (to Cliff)
    What are you doing?

                  CLIFF
    Nothin'. I just thought that it was
    interesting hearing Torrance's
    point of view.

                  MISSY
    How do you even know her?

                  CLIFF
    We're old friends.

                  TORRANCE
    Ever been to a cheerleading
    competition?

                  MISSY
    Oh, you mean like a football game?

                  TORRANCE
    No, not a game. Those are like
    practices for us. I'm talking about
    a tournament. ESPN cameras all
    around, hundreds of people in the
    crowds cheering.

                  CLIFF
    Wait. People cheering cheerleaders?

                  TORRANCE
    That's right. Lots of people.
    Here's the deal, Missy. We're the
    shit. The best. We have fun, we
    work hard, and we win national
    championships. I'm offering you a
    chance to be a part of that.

Torrance sizes Missy up.

                  CLIFF
           (mock encouraging)
    Think about it, Miss. You get to
    wear sassy outfits. You get to yell
    like you care about something.
           (to Torrance)
    She's not the cheering type.

Missy glares at Cliff, then looks at Torrance, debating.

                  MISSY
    You know what? Count me in.

25.

Torrance smiles.

INT GYMNASIUM - DAY

The Squad goes through their routine: As Torrance and the
squad hit the floor for practice, Missy sits on the
sidelines.

>   TORRANCE
>   Ready, girls? I said, Brrrrrr It's
>   cold in here, I guess there must be
>   some Toros in the atmosphere / I
>   said brrr It's cold in here / I
>   said there must be some Toros in
>   the atmosphere. / I said oh-ee, oh-
>   ee, oh lce, ice, ice / Oh-ee, oh-
>   ee, oh lce, ice, ice. Here we go,
>   girls.

ECU: BOOMBOX SPEAKER/MUSIC: "LET ME CLEAR MY THROAT"

As she watches, Missy's expression starts to change. She
recognizes something. The words, the moves -- she's seen them
somewhere.

Then something CLICKS -- and she looks pissed. She quickly
gets up and storms out of the gym.

The squad members look at teach other, then at Torrance.
Courtney and Whitney step forward.

>   COURTNEY
>   Nice recruit, Torrance. A real
>   captain would've seen what I saw: a
>   big dykey loser.

>   WHITNEY
>   I'd say that's strike two.

Torrance is PISSED.

EXT. GYMNASIUM - MOMENTS LATER

Missy is at her car, about to hop in, when Torrance catches
up to her.

>   TORRANCE
>   What the hell is up? I went out on
>   a limb for you, and you just bail?

96

                    MISSY
               (equally pissed)
          I'm not about stealing.

                    TORRANCE
          What are you talking about?

                    MISSY
          You ripped off those cheers.

                    TORRANCE
          Listen, Missy, our cheers are 100%
          original. Count the trophies.

                    MISSY
          Well, your trophies are bullshit,
          because you're a sad-ass liar.

                    TORRANCE
          All right, that's it! Get out of
          the car! I'm gonna kick your ass!

                    MISSY
          Oh, really?

Missy steps out of the car and gets in Torrance's face.

                    TORRANCE
          Come on.

                    MISSY
          You're in for a rude awakening.

It's a standoff. And just when we think Missy might throw a
punch, she motions toward her car.

                    MISSY   (CONT'D)
               (continuing)
          Get in.

                    TORRANCE
          What? No way.

Missy hops in the drivers' side, a slight smile on her face.

                    MISSY
          For real. Get in.

Torrance mulls it over. She looks back toward the gym. Then
at the car. Something tells her to trust Missy.

She gets in the car.

INT. EAST COMPTON HS GYMNASIUM - NIGHT

The MASCOT is an orange leprechaun picking a green four-leaf clover. Ancient, the fourth leaf has cracked and is hanging on by a thread.

A PEP RALLY is in progress. The SPECTATORS start stomping and WHISTLING.

SEVEN GIRLS and SEVEN GUYS - the predominantly African-American and Hispanic East Compton Clover Cheerleading Squad wear hip green and orange uniforms. They're LAUGHING, elbowing each other, having fun.

The CAPTAIN, raises her arms like a conductor. Her squad falls silent.

                    ISIS
          I said: Brrrrrrrrrr, it's cold in
          here, I guess there must be some
          Clovers in the atmosphere. I say
          Brrrrrrrrrr, it's cold in here, I
          said there must be some Clovers in
          the at-mo-sphere. I said: ice,
          ice, ice! Ohweohweoh! Ice, ice,
          ice! Ohweohweoh!

Torrance and Missy watch from outside the gym. Torrance is shocked.

The entire CLOVER SQUAD begins a Byzantine stepping sequence featuring INTRICATE STOMPING & CLAPPING RHYTHMS.

'LET ME CLEAR MY THROAT' begins and the squad launches into a fierce dance sequence. It's the original (and more complex) version of the routine the Toros just did. Only better. MUCH, MUCH, BETTER.

SLO MO on Torrance, stunned.

EXT. COMPTON HS PARKING LOT - NIGHT

As she and Missy head to the car, Torrance is rattled and on the verge of tears. Missy watches her.

Suddenly Isis appears. She has TWO CLOVER COHORTS, LA FRED and JENELOPE.

                    ISIS
          Hey! You guys enjoy the show?

                    JENELOPE
Yes, were the ethnic festivities to
your liking today?

                    TORRANCE
You guys are awesome.

                    ISIS
        (dripping)
Really? You're ready to share those
trophies?

                    JENELOPE
Can we just beat these Buffy's down
so I can go home? I'm on curfew,
girl.

                    MISSY
Look, there's no need for that.

                    ISIS
Oh, you know what? She's right.
See, then we'd be doing them a
favor. See, then they could feel
good about sending Raggedy Ann up
here to jack us for our cheers.

                    TORRANCE
Raggedy Ann?

                    ISIS
Ugly redhead with a video camera
permanently attached to her hand?
Ya'll have been comin' up here for
years tryin to steal our routines.

                    LAFRED
And we just love seein' them on
ESPN.

                    TORRANCE
What are you talking about?

                    ISIS
"Brr it's cold in here? There must
be some Toros in the atmosphere?" I
know you don't think a white girl
made that up?

                    TORRANCE
I.. I really..

                                        99

                    ISIS
          Our free cheer service is over as
          of this moment.

                    JENELOPE
          Over!

                    LAFRED
          Finito!

                    ISIS
          God, it's like everytime we get
          some, here y'all come, trying to
          steal it, putting blonde hair on it
          and calling it something different.
          We've had the best squad around for
          years, but no one's been able to
          see what we can do. Oh, but you
          better believe all that's gonna
          change this year. I'm captain, and
          I guarantee you we will make it to
          nationals. So, just hand over the
          tape you made tonight and we'll
          call it even for now.

                    TORRANCE
          We don't have any tape.

                    MISSY
          Really. We just came to see the
          show.

                    JENELOPE
          What? Come on, Isis. Let me do
          this.

     Isis sizes them up. It's a tense moment. Then..

                    ISIS
          You know what? Let's go.

                    JENELOPE
          Wait a minute. So that's it? We're
          just gonna let them go?

                    ISIS
          Yeah, because unlike them, we have
          class.

                    TORRANCE
          I swear I had no idea.

                    ISIS
          Well, now you do.

                    JENELOPE
          Hmmph. You been touched by an
          angel, girl.

Torrance and Missy back away and head for the car.

INT. MISSY'S CAR - NIGHT

                    MISSY
          We just so almost got our asses
          kicked back there! I mean, I knew
          I'd seen those routines before. We
          used to play East Compton all the
          time.

Torrance is really shattered. Missy registers this.

                    MISSY (CONT'D)
          You really had no idea, did you?

                    TORRANCE
          Do you know what this means? My
          entire cheerleading career has been
          a lie.

                    MISSY
          Well, look on the bright side. It's
          only cheerleading.

                    TORRANCE
          I am only cheerleading.

Missy looks at her and sees that she means it.

                    TORRANCE (CONT'D)
          Do you believe in curses?

                    MISSY
          What are you talking about?

                    TORRANCE
          I think I'm cursed.

                    MISSY
          And why is that?

                    TORRANCE
          This past summer at cheer camp, all
          the new seniors had to do a dare.
          See, there's this thing called the
          Spirit Stick, and it can never,
          ever touch the ground.

31.

SCARY MUSIC swells as we...

INT. CAMP LOCATION CAFETERIA - NIGHT

ECU: The Spirit Stick

                    BIG RED
          Torrance Shipman, your mission,
          should you choose to accept it -
          and you better - is to capture the
          Spirit Stick...

Big Red eyes the other squad members with an evil grin.

                    BIG RED (CONT'D)
          ...and drop it in front of the
          entire camp.

Torrance is appalled, looking like she just watched someone
eat their own barf, grudgingly heading over to the winning
team.

ANGLE ON: THE SPIRIT STICK

Perched atop an ornate tufted pillow, the Spirit Stick holds
court on its' throne. A brightly painted broom handle, it is
covered with RHINESTONES and emanating celestial light.

The New Pope SQUAD is excited to see her, greeting Torrance
with Southern syrup.

                    NEW POPE CHEERLEADER #1
          Y'all are such an inspiration to
          us.

                    TORRANCE
          Well, I just wanted to congratulate
          you guys and take a picture of
          you... with the Spirit Stick.

The squad hits an ornate formation in seconds flat. Torrance
grabs the Stick, handing it over.

                    TORRANCE (CONT'D)
          Here --

Accidentally/on-purpose, Torrance passes the Stick too
quickly, letting it fall --

IN SLO MO: As New Pope girls fly through the air - as if the
stick is a grenade - to prevent it from touching the ground.

NEW POPE FACES distort in genuine horror, silent screams of
agony, as the Spirit Stick hits the floor with an echoing
CRACK, RIBBONS and SEQUINS flying everywhere.

IN REAL TIME: The mess hall is quiet as the collective GASPS
OF HORROR, OUTRAGE, and SHOCK reverb through the room.

Torrance picks up the Stick and attempts to hand it to a
nervous New Pope cheerleader.

                    TORRANCE (CONT'D)
          Here.

                    NEW POPE CHEERLEADER #1
          I don't want it now.

                    NEW POPE CHEERLEADER #2
          No, it's okay. The Spirit Stick
          doesn't lose anything. The person
          who drops it, however, goes to
          Hades!

INT. MISSY'S CAR - NIGHT

Torrance is stricken. Missy bursts out laughing.

                    MISSY
          I don't mean to laugh, but
          cheerleading urban legend?

Nodding, Torrance means business. Missy's incredulous.

                    MISSY (CONT'D)
          You're not jinxed. Shit happens.

EXT. FREEWAY - NIGHT

Missy's car blazes back to San Diego.

INT. SHIPMAN LIVING ROOM - NIGHT

Torrance enters ashen-faces and makes a beeline for the
phone. Justin rushes after her.

                    JUSTIN
          Hey, I have to tell you something.

                    TORRANCE
          I'm on the phone, creep.

                    JUSTIN
          I realize that, and normally I'd be
          listening on the other line, but
          this is important.

                    TORRANCE
          Okay, what?

Justin promptly jumps up, sticks his butt in her face, and
farts loudly.

                    TORRANCE   (CONT'D)
               (raging)
          Ohh! Get out!

                    JUSTIN
          Thank you for listening.

Torrance dials.

                    GUY ON PHONE
          Yo.

                    TORRANCE
          Is Aaron around?

                    GUY ON PHONE
          Back later.

                    TORRANCE
          Do you know when?

                    GUY ON PHONE
          No.

                    TORRANCE
          Have him call Torrance. It's
          urgent.

                    GUY ON PHONE
          All right.

Torrance throws the phone down and stomps in a rage.

                    TORRANCE
          Big Red totally screwed us!

EXT. FOOTBALL FIELD - NEXT DAY

Torrance has clearly dropped the bomb. The squad is taking
it in, while Missy, Jan and Les form the central chorus.

                    TORRANCE
          I mean monster screwed us! I put
          this to the entire squad. Swear you
          guys didn't know.

The entire squad GRUMBLE and GASP denials.

                    JAN
          Big Red didn't exactly let any of
          us help with the routines,
          Torrance.

                    LES
          I cannot believe she did this.

                    TORRANCE
          I feel awful. It's depraved. I
          mean, those East Compton girls
          wanted to grill our asses.

                    DARCY
          Big Red ran the show, man. We were
          just flying ignorami, for sobbing
          out loud.

                    TORRANCE
          We can't go to regionals with a
          stolen routine. It's too risky.

                    WHITNEY
          Changing the routine now would be
          total murder-suicide.

                    COURTNEY
          Seriously. Let's not put the "duh"
          in "dumb."

Courtney looks at Whitney, who nods.

                    DARCY
          How are East Compton gonna prove
          anything?

                    MISSY
          You people are unbelievable. I
          mean, we're talking about cheating
          here.

                    COURTNEY
          Sorry, new girl, but nobody hit
          your buzzer.

Courtney stands dramatically, commanding everyone's
attention.

35.

                    COURTNEY (CONT'D)
          Look, I hate to be predictable, but
          I don't give a shit. We learned
          that routine fair and square. We
          logged the man-hours. Don't punish
          the squad for Big Red's mistake.
          This isn't about cheating. This is
          about winning.
                    (raising her hand)
          Everyone in favor of winning?

The entire squad raises their hands, with the exception of
Torrance and Missy, who exchange a look.

                    TORRANCE
          I get what you're saying, Missy,
          but there's no time. If we don't do
          the routine, we've got nothing
          else.

                    JAN
          So, you in?

Missy rolls her eyes, pissed.

                    MISSY
          Whatever.

EXT. SHIPMAN HOUSE - DUSK - ESTABLISHING

O.S. The SOUND of a DIAL TONE, followed by the sound of AUTO-
DIAL, followed by a BUSY SIGNAL.

INT. SHIPMAN LIVING ROOM - CONTINUOUS

PHONE filling frame. Finger hits speakerphone. AUTO-DIAL.
BUSY SIGNAL. Hang up. Speakerphone, auto-dial BUSY SIGNAL,
hang-up.

Torrance mans the phone. A sprawled-out Justin plays Sega.
Stacks of college applications share the coffee table with
the phone.

                    TORRANCE
          Get out of here!

                    JUSTIN
          Hey, this is the living room. It's
          public domain.

The phone rings. Over speakerphone, we hear a VOICE answer.

                    GUY ON PHONE (O.S)
          Yo.

Torrance snatches up the phone.

                    TORRANCE
          Hey, may I please speak to Aaron?
          It's Torrance.

                    GUY ON PHONE
          He's not here. He's, uh- He's not
          here. Bye.

Suddenly the phone erupts into that awful PHONE-OFF-THE-HOOK
NOISE. Justin cracks up.

                    TORRANCE
              (flustered)
          Ohh!

                    JUSTIN
          I'll take "Famous Losers" for $200
          Alex.

                    TORRANCE
          Shut up, moron!

                    JUSTIN
          It's not my fault you're in love
          with a big gay cheerleader who
          won't return your phone calls.

                    TORRANCE
          Aaron is not gay.

                    JUSTIN
          Oh, so someone just made him become
          a cheerleader?

                    TORRANCE
          He's just... busy!

                    JUSTIN
          Yeah, busy scamming on guys.

                    TORRANCE
          Give me that!

Torrance rips the video game controller out of Justin's
hands.

                    JUSTIN
          Bitch!

EXT. PANTONE HOUSE - NIGHT

Torrance, Les, and Jan pull up in uniform, commanding in
Les's '72 SUBURBAN. HONK. Anxious, they wait to see Missy in
her uniform.

                    LES
          Where is she? Come on.

Missy finally opens the door, embarrassed at first, but after
hearing their hoots and hollars she does a sexy dance for the
crew in the car.

                    TORRANCE / LES / JAN
          Sexy mama! Whoo! Take it off! Come
          on. Go, sexy. Whoo! You're on fire,
          yeah!

INT. LES' CAR - NIGHT

                    TORRANCE
          You sure I can stay over your house
          tonight?

                    MISSY
          Totally fine. My parents are at
          some benefit. They'll be pouring
          themselves into bed around dawn.

                    TORRANCE
          Good. We gotta start early. You'll
          be a star cheerleader yet.

                    JAN
          You know, all the cheerleaders in
          the world wouldn't help our
          football team.

                    LES
          Man, it's just wrong. Cheering for
          them is just plain mean.

                    JAN
          Everybody comes to see you ladies,
          anyway.

                    MISSY
          Because we're such fine athletes.

                    JAN
          Oh, live with it. You'll be
          fighting off major oglers while we
          defend our sexuality.

                    MISSY
               (beat)
          What is your sexuality?

                    LES
          Well, Jan's straight, while I'm...
          controversial.

                    MISSY
               (to Les)
          Are you trying to tell me you speak
          fag?

                    LES
          Oh, fluently.

                    MISSY
          And Courtney and Whitney, "dyke-
          adelic"?

                    TORRANCE
          No!

                    LES
          Are you kidding?

                    JAN
          I don't think so. See, um, Courtney
          doesn't wear anything under her
          spankies.

                    LES
          That's no excuse, Jan.

Jan and Les choke on chuckles.

                    JAN
          I can't help it if my digits slip
          occasionally.

                    MISSY
          Nuh-uh. Slip? Where?

                    LES
          Come on, Missy. Don't make him say
          it.

                    MISSY
          Oh, my God.

                    JAN
          My God, too.

                    LES
      You're a sick man, Jan.

EXT. FOOTBALL FIELD - NIGHT

Torrance and company cruise the sidelines, waving to people
and generally ruling the proceedings.

                    ANNOUNCER
          Now, ladies and gentlemen, put your
          hands together for the Rancho Carne
          Toros!

FOOTBALL

          And now, without further ado, let's
          hear it for the five-time National
          Cheerleading Champions, the mighty
          Toros!

BAND goes nuts. CROWD does the WAVE.

MISSY gets her bearings while IN THE STANDS, Cliff shakes his
head, reading *THE NAKED APE*.

                    SQUAD
          Go! Go! Come on! We're number one!
          Come on! Let's hear it! Whoo! Yeah!
          Bring it on, baby! Come on! Let's
          hear it! Go, Toros! Come on, Toros!
          Whoo! Go, Toros! Come on, Toros!
          Come on. Yeah! Yeah, Toros! Yeah!
          Go, Toros! Yo-ho, go, everybody!

CENTERFIELD

The COSTA MESA CO-CAPTAINS and the RCH CO-CAPTAINS meet for
the coin toss. The REF takes his time.

                    FOOTBALL PLAYER #1
          Why don't you let your cheerleaders
          play for you? At least they win
          shit occasionally.

                    RCH QUARTERBACK
          Is that the best you got?

                    RCH TIGHT END
          Yeah, come on, bring it on, butt
          plug.

                    FOOTBALL PLAYER #1
          You want more? Okay. While we're
          out here kicking your ass, your
          cheer boys are over there scamming
          on all your squirrel.

                    FOOTBALL PLAYER #2
          Which is cool, since you don't have
          dicks anyway.

                    FOOTBALL PLAYER #1
          Mm-hmm.

                    RCH QUARTERBACK
          Bitch!

                    RCH TIGHT END
          Punk!

RCH Quarterback shoves the Costa Mesa Linebacker with fury.
Costa Mesa Linebacker shoves him back, the Tight End and CMQB
getting into the pile-up. The REF tosses the yellow flag,
blowing the WHISTLE.

EXT. SIDELINES - CONTINUOUS

ON THE SQUAD reacting to the melee. Courtney adjusts her
spanky pants. Jan looks at her. She bends over to tie her
cheer-sneaks, knowing full-well that he's looking.

ON JAN ogling.

ON COURTNEY smiling broadly at Jan while tying her laces.

ON THE FIELD: The SEVEN VISITING CHEERLEADERS do their 'HELLO
CHEER. The SQUAD turning, raising their skirts, revealing
letters spelling: 'YOU SUCK!'

                    VISITING SQUAD
          Hey, Toros / That's right / The
          red, black and white / Guess what,
          guess what / You really suck!

74   ON THE SIDELINES, FDS CHEERLEADERS explode with a response.74

                    TOROS
          Hey, that's all right / That's okay
          / You're gonna pump our gas someday
          / That's all right / That's okay /
          You're gonna pump our gas someday!

ON THE FIELD the REFEREE blows the WHISTLE. The GAME begins.

                                                              111

EXT. BLEACHERS - CONTINUOUS

                    TORRANCE
          Come on, guys! Touchdown! Let's go,
          yeah!

- RCH Quarterback is immediately TACKLED.

                    CLIFF
          Nice.

- SPECTATORS wincing from relentless painful tackles.

                    ANNOUNCER (O.S.)
          Fourteen-nothing.

                    CROWD
          Go!

                    RCH FOOTBALL PLAYER
          Hut!

                    ANNOUNCER (O.S.)
          And with 4:50 left in the third
          quarter...

                    TORRANCE
          Losers.

                    ANNOUNCER (O.S.)
          ...it's Costa Mesa, 34. Toros,
          nothing.

                    SQUAD
          Come on, Defense, work!

                    CROWD
          Work!

ON TORRANCE noticing Cliff as SPECTATORS join.

                    SQUAD
          Knock 'em down, roll 'em around.
          Come on, Defense, work!

                    CROWD
          Work!

                    SQUAD
          Knock 'em down, roll 'em around.
          Come on, Defense, work!

Cliff making eye contact -- and waves.

                    CROWD
     Work!

                    SQUAD
     Knock 'em down, roll 'em around.
     Come on, Defense, work!

                    CROWD
     Work!

Whitney and Courtney clocking the obvious chemistry.

                    SQUAD
     Knock 'em down, roll 'em around.
     Come on, Defense, work!

                    CROWD
     Work!

                    SQUAD
     Knock 'em down, roll 'em around.
     Come on, Defense, work!

COURTNEY AND JAN do the same lift. As Courtney nails her
'chair', her eyes pop out. Jan grins wolfishly, his hand
clearly holding her by the butt.

                    COURTNEY
     Oh! Ooh!

Courtney WHOOPS and jumps out of her stunt early, thwacking
him.

                    COURTNEY (CONT'D)
     Jan!

Jan admires his thumb and cheers.

                    JAN
     Go, Toros! Come on! Yeah! Come on,
     Toros!

Cliff grinning at Torrance. Whitney and Courtney seizing the
moment.

                    WHITNEY
     You're, like, totally his eye
     candy.

                    COURTNEY
     God, I can't believe you'd do that
     to Aaron.

43.

                    TORRANCE
          Do what?

                    WHITNEY
          Especially with him.

                    TORRANCE
          What are you talking about?

                    WHITNEY
          Oh, don't play dumb. We're better
          at it than you.

                    COURTNEY
          You're having cheer sex with him.

Torrance frowns and gives one last look at Cliff in the
bleachers.

                    ANNOUNCER (O.S.)
          Flag on the play, called against-
          you guessed it- the Toros.
          Remember, our next defeat is
          scheduled for next Friday night at
          8:00.

78   ANGLE ON the bleacher entrance as ISIS and CLOVERS calms the   78
          posse with a reassuring look.

                    SQUAD/CROWD
          Let's go, Toros! Let's go, Toros!
          Let's go, Toros! Let's go, Toros!
          Let's go, Toros! All right!

In the glow of the night game lights, ISIS & THREE CLOVER
CHEERLEADERS commanding bleachers right above the Toros.

                    SQUAD
          We're sweet / We got the whip / We
          can't be beat. / We're the best /
          Our team's too cool / We got the
          class to rock this school / Ah,
          yeah!

EAST COMPTON and RCH are now face to face, in show-down mode.
A human group mirror, both squads perform the cheers. The
Clovers mimic the RCH chant perfectly.

                    CLOVERS
          We bad, we got the team / We can't
          be had / We're the best / So score
          them points / You win the game /
          We'll rock this joint.

The AUDIENCE is enraptured with this show-down, VARIOUS
REACTIONS from VARIOUS CROWD-MEMBERS.

> SQUAD
> Go, Toros, go, Toros. Go, go, go,
> Toros.

Isis' group dominate the cheer in a deliverance-style case of
one-upmanship. The Clovers turn and face the audience.

> CLOVERS
> Go, Clovers, go, Clovers. Go, go,
> go, Clovers.

The entire RCH squad gets tighter and louder in response. The
Clovers rise to the challenge of being outnumbered: They are
fierce.

> CLOVERS/SQUAD
> Our game is fierce and we are hip /
> So get on back / You can't touch
> this / Our game is bad / We're
> without peer / So get that weakness
> outta here.
> (beat)
> Tried to steal our bit but you look
> like shit / But we're the ones who
> are down with it.

The Clovers exit with a flourish. Our squad looks at each
other, totally busted.

> COURTNEY
> (indignant)
> I still say we use the routine we
> have. If we have to start over, I
> quit.

The game BUZZER sounds. RCH has lost. The scoreboard reads 42-
0. The squad gives Courtney a collective eye-roll.

> ANNOUNCER (O.S.)
> And that's the game. Final score.
> 34: Cougars, Toros: nothing.

> TORRANCE
> Whoever here is for a new routine,
> raise your hand.

Everyone - including the BYSTANDERS in the stands - RAISE
THEIR HANDS.

Several RCH football players, freshly defeated, walk by.

45.

> RCH QUARTERBACK
> Jan's got spirit. Yes, he do.

> RCH TIGHT END
> Jan's got spirit. How 'bout you?

Jan can't even fathom that they have the gall at this moment.

> JAN
> Dude, you just lost.

INT. PANTONE HOUSE - NIGHT

Missy and Torrance getting ready for bed.

> MISSY
> So is every game that eventful?

> TORRANCE
> No, thank God. We have a real
> situation on our hands. I mean, we
> were humiliated on our own turf.

> MISSY
> We might have to have a rumble.

> TORRANCE
> This is a serious problem!

> MISSY
> Oh, so is your breath.

> TORRANCE
> Oh, my God.

> MISSY
> Yeah.

Torrance grabs her toothbrush and heads to the bathroom.
GUITAR RIFFS --

EXT./INT. CLIFF'S ROOM - BACK AND FORTH

-- distorting through an AMP. Torrance peeking into Cliff's
room from the HALL, while Cliff is wildly strumming his
electric guitar.

Torrance gazing in amusement, also a little impressed. BEHIND
HER, Missy appears.

> MISSY (CONT'D)
> What are you doing?

Torrance blushing in embarrassment, busted peeping on Cliff.

                    TORRANCE
               (recovering)
          Um... Where's the bathroom?

                    MISSY
          Right there.

                    TORRANCE
          Oh.

ON MISSY grossed out by her brother.

ON CLIFF punctuating the attention with a LICK.

INT. BATHROOM - NIGHT

Cliff joins Torrance at the sink, totally sidling up to her.
Torrance is coyly trying to cover.

Cliff unscrews the toothpaste cap, squeezing the toothpaste
onto the bristles. He turns on the water. She rinses,
shutting it off. He turns the faucet back on. She rinses,
shutting it off. She spits. He spits. A playful interlude,
bursting with romantic tension. He rinses and spits again,
wiping his mouth and giving her a huge smile before exiting.

INT. MISSY'S BEDROOM

Torrance switches off the light, crawling into bed next to
Missy and pulling the covers up. Missy's contemplative.

                    TORRANCE
          Good night.

OVERHEAD on Torrance and Missy.

                    MISSY
          Night. Are you into my brother?

                    TORRANCE
               (yes)
          No. I have a boyfriend.

ON TORRANCE, turning her head, thinking of CLIFF.

MATCH DISSOLVE to CLIFF, likely thinking of Torrance with a
smile.

INT. AARON'S DORM ROOM - NEXT MORNING

The phone RINGS. Aaron sits up in bed.

                    AARON
          Hello?

                    TORRANCE (V.O.)
          Aaron?

                    AARON
          Tor, is that you?

INT. MISSY'S BEDROOM - INTERCUT

Torrance fretting and pacing by Missy's bed impatiently.

                    TORRANCE
          Where have you been? I keep trying
          to call you.

                    AARON
          Yeah, I know. I've been, like,
          totally busy with school and
          practice and stuff. What's up?

                    TORRANCE
          Oh, it's bad, Aaron. Miss Red
          snaked our routines from the East
          Compton Clovers. All of our
          routines.

                    AARON
          What?

                    TORRANCE
          They found out. They showed up at
          the game. Gauntlets were thrown.
          Tell me you didn't know about this.
          I mean, I don't know what to do
          here.

                    AARON
          Of course I didn't know, but you
          gotta calm down. This is not that
          big a deal. Everybody uses
          everybody else's material. It's
          like this unwritten rule or
          something.

                         TORRANCE
          That doesn't help me. We can't do
          their routine at Regionals because
          they're gonna do their routine at
          Regionals.

                         AARON
          Come on, Tor, you need a new
          routine. That's all. No problem.
          Just hire a professional
          choreographer.

                         TORRANCE (O.S.)
          A choreographer?

                         AARON (O.S.)
          Look, just think of it as
          collaboration. The U.C.A. totally
          looks the other way. Call this guy.
          His name is Sparky Polastri.

                         TORRANCE
               (to Missy)
          Pen.

                         AARON
          Met him at nationals last year?
          Knows his shit, all right? Here's
          the number. It's 555-7219.

                         TORRANCE
          Thanks, Aaron. You always know what
          to do.

WIDER REVEALING a RANDOM GIRL in Aaron's bed.

                         AARON
          Mm-hmm. Bye, baby.

                         RANDOM GIRL
          Mmm, who was that?

                         AARON
          My sister. Mmm. But you're not my
          sister, are you?

INT. MISSY'S BEDROOM - MOMENTS LATER

Hanging up, Torrance looks at Missy, who is dressing. Missy
shrugs. Torrance is still in her P.J.'s as she sits cross-
legged on the bed.

49.

> TORRANCE
> He says we should hire a
> choreographer.

Torrance dials the phone. It rings.

> SPARKY POLASTRI (V.O.)
> Hello.

> TORRANCE
> Hi. May I please speak to Sparky
> Polastri?

EXT. RCH HALLWAY - DAY

Torrance cornering Darcy and Kasey by their lockers.

> TORRANCE
> He'll need three or four days to
> teach us the routine.

> KASEY
> But here's the thing. It's gonna
> cost us 2000 dollars.

> DARCY
> What, do I have the letters A-T-M
> tattooed on my forehead?

> TORRANCE
> We were thinking more like D-A-D-D-
> Y.

> DARCY
> Maybe I can get $500.

> TORRANCE
> Okay, then we only need $1500 more
> by Monday.

A CLASS BELL becomes the sound of BRAKES SCREECHING as --

EXT. CAR WASH - DAY

Whitney poses in a bikini holding a sign that reads: CAR WASH
$15. A LINE OF CARS waits to get their lab dance, uh, cars
washed.

The TOROS are busy sudsing and hosing off cars. In bikinis.

SLO MO water spraying. Everyone running around with squirt
guns. Les catching it all on video.

120

LES
What's up, Whitney?

WHITNEY
Hi.

LES
Here we are at the Rancho Carne
Toro car wash, raising a little
money. Yeah, baby, yeah! Work it,
Kasey!

Les pointing the camera at Courtney.

COURTNEY
Come to Mama.

LES
Soak it up.

VARIOUS FUN SHOTS of CAR WASH and TOROS.

LES (CONT'D)
Oh, that's attractive, Tor.

LES (CONT'D)
Lookin'good. Shakin' the booty.
(now on Missy)
Missy, what the hell are you doing?

Missy violently strokes the car's antenna up and down in a
nerdy fashion.

A WATER FIGHT breaks out. Les gets dunked with a bucket of
water from behind.

LES (CONT'D)
Watch it! Aww! Dude, watch out for
the camera!

Cliff walks up, and is instantly drawn to Torrance, who he
watches from afar.

MISSY
Hey, perv.

Startled, Cliff turns to find his bikini-clad sister.

MISSY (CONT'D)
Hand over your 15 bucks or get out
of here.

CLIFF
What are you doing?

> MISSY
> Making money from guys ogling my
> goodies.

> CLIFF
> Aw, I didn't need to hear that.
> That was an over-share.

> MISSY
> (to Torrance)
> Hey, Torrance. Come here a sec.

Torrance heading over, happy to see Cliff.

> MISSY (CONT'D)
> (to Cliff)
> We'll just get this over with.
> (to Torrance)
> My brother wants to check out your
> rack.

Blushing, Torrance folds her arms over her chest.

> CLIFF
> You know, I begged my mom for a
> brother.

> TORRANCE
> He'd look a little ridiculous in
> that bikini, wouldn't he?

> CLIFF
> Yeah.

> TORRANCE
> So, nice car.

Torrance pointing to a muddy car behind Cliff, that appears
to be shaped like a car.

> CLIFF
> Yeah. Um- What can I say? I drive
> hard.

> TORRANCE
> Shouldn't take long to wash.

> CLIFF
> Don't even worry about it. I got
> all afternoon.

> TORRANCE
> I'll bet you do.

INT. GYMNASIUM - DAY

SQUAD is warming up, waiting for the choreographer.

                    COURTNEY
          Where the hell is this guy?

                    TORRANCE
          Listen, we're lucky he's even doing
          this for us.

The door opens, suddenly, and their eyes widen upon seeing:

SPARKY POLASTRI! His outfit consists of all black. He places
an audiocassette in the deck and stands at attention in
themiddle of the room, eyes closed in meditation.

Torrance, Missy, Jan and Les steal a concerned look. An AUDIO
BITE sounds:

                    AUDIO BITE (O.S.)
          "Prepare for total domination --"

As what we'll call 'SPARKY's THEME' begins, Sparky launches
into a series of moves. This is followed by some very
'white-guy-trying-to-be-funky' choreography. The music is
way behind the curve, and Sparky is way too into it. Addingun-
necessary theatrical touches, Sparky Polastri is 'Lord of the
Dance.'

ON THE SQUAD, queasy from the horror.

                    TORRANCE
          Thanks for coming. We're-

                    SPARKY
          Don't speak.

Sparky begins tearing the squad down. First KASEY.

                    SPARKY (CONT'D)
          You. You have weak ankles.

Then WHITNEY.

                    SPARKY (CONT'D)
          One of your calves is bigger than
          the other.
                    (dismissive)
          Too much makeup. Not enough makeup.

On COURTNEY.

>   SPARKY (CONT'D)
>   What's with the skin? Say it with
>   me: "Sunlight"!

JAN AND LES.

>   SPARKY (CONT'D)
>   Male cheerleaders. Enough said.

ON MISSY.

>   SPARKY (CONT'D)
>   Smile.

Missy smiles.

>   SPARKY (CONT'D)
>   Don't smile.

>   MISSY
>   Jackass.

ON DARCY.

>   SPARKY
>   Good general tone and musculature.
>   Report those continents to your ass
>   before it gets so big... it forms
>   its own website.

And finally ON TORRANCE.

>   SPARKY (CONT'D)
>   And you. I take you to be the
>   captain, which means you'll
>   probably need more work than
>   anyone.

>   TORRANCE
>   Look, you don't-

>   SPARKY
>   (finger to her lips)
>   Shh!

>   TORRANCE
>   But-

>   SPARKY
>   No, no, no. Don't speak. Don't
>   think. Listen and learn.

SPARKY surveyng and holding court imperiously.

Watching Sparky with dismayed wonder, Torrance, Missy, Jan and Les successfully imitating deer caught in headlights.

> SPARKY (CONT'D)
> I'm a choreographer. That's what I do. You... are cheerleaders. Cheerleaders are dancers who have gone retarded. What you do is a tiny, pathetic subset of dancing. I will attempt to transform your robotic routines into poetry... written with the human body. Follow me or perish, sweater monkeys.

Courtney and Whitney glaring at Torrance. The squad is now warming up.

> SPARKY (CONT'D)
> I want you to think of what you ate today. Got it? Now cut that in half. This is called a diet. Everyone start one today. Darcy, honey, you should stop eating. You see, when you skip a meal, your body feeds off its fat stores. And if you skip enough, maybe your body will eat your ass.

> COURTNEY
> Why does everyone have to go on a diet?

> SPARKY
> Because in cheerleading, we throw people in the air, and fat people don't go as high. Come on, come on. Let's get back to work!

Missy is being thrown in the air, with Jan spotting her.

> SPARKY (CONT'D)
> Ah! I want dangerous! I wanna feel like somebody's gonna snap their neck! Spirit fingers! Give me spirit fingers! Spirit fingers. Give me spirit!

As Jan barely catches her - by the shorts - giving her a major wedgie. Missy SWATS him.

> MISSY
> Ouch!

                         JAN
              What? I told you I'd catch you.

Furious, Missy's digging her underwear out of her ass. Sparky
puts a hand on her shoulder, very solemn.

                        SPARKY
              Look, I understand you have
              underwear up your ass right now,
              but it beats the hell out of a
              shattered skull. Think about it.
                    (then)
              Okay, now, spirit fingers. Spirit
              fingers! And spirit fingers!

The SQUAD wiggling their "spirit fingers" to Sparky's
mortification.

                       TORRANCE
              Oh, my God!

                        SPARKY
              These are not spirit fingers.

Sparky's demonstrating correct "spirit fingers" technique.

                   SPARKY (CONT'D)
              These are spirit fingers. And
              these...are gold.

EXT. MISSY'S BACKYARD - DAY

Torrance and Missy practice the new routine together.

                   TORRANCE/MISSY
              One, two, three, four, five, six,
              seven, eight. One, two, three,
              four, five, six, seven, eight.

                         MISSY
              Screw this. I did not sign on for
              spirit fingers.

                       TORRANCE
              Come on! The spirit fingers are
              great!

Missy runs off and goes inside.

                         MISSY
              Yeah, whatever.

Torrance sways on the big swing, she looks fried.

                    TORRANCE
              (sitting on a swing)
          We are so screwed.

Cliff approaches.

                    CLIFF
          Hey. What's the matter?

                    TORRANCE
          Hey. You don't wanna know.

                    CLIFF
          Ah. Cheer crisis.

                    TORRANCE
          I've just gotten so bogged down in
          all this... crap.

                    CLIFF
          Well, if it's crap, why do you do
          it?

Torrance laughs. Cliff pushing Torrance on the swing.

                    TORRANCE
          I don't know.

                    CLIFF
          So quit.

                    TORRANCE
          Maybe I should.

                    CLIFF
          Yeah, I mean, if you don't like it
          anymore.

                    TORRANCE
          I didn't say that.

                    CLIFF
          Sounds like it.

                    TORRANCE
          I don't know what I want.

                    CLIFF
          I remember back when I cheered at
          my school in Detroit.

                    TORRANCE
          You cheered at your other high
          school?

>   CLIFF
>   No, I never cheered, but I know
>   what you're going through. And
>   regardless of all the politics and
>   the doubts... and the crap, you
>   just have to know that you can do
>   it. And if it helps, I know you
>   can.

Torrance ponders this, nodding and smiling.

>   TORRANCE
>   (sweetly)
>   You do?

>   CLIFF
>   Yeah.

They gaze into each other's eyes, and are about to kiss.
Missy re-emerging as Torrance and Cliff quickly pull away.

>   MISSY
>   All right, all right! I'm ready to
>   make a fool of myself. State
>   regionals, here we come.

EXT. CAL STATE DOMINGUEZ HILLS - DAY - ESTABLISHING

INT. CAL STATE REGIONALS/REGISTRATION AREA - DAY

We see, for the first time: the HUGE CROWD. With THUMPING
MUSIC in background, HUNDREDS of CHEER and DANCE SQUADS mill
about. The Toros enter, taking in all of the commotion and
going different ways, Missy and Torrance walk in together.

>   TORRANCE
>   Welcome to the world of competitive
>   cheerleading.

An EVENT COORDINATOR with a clipboard directs traffic like
she's helming an aircraft carrier. In combat.

>   EVENT COORDINATOR
>   High school divisions, please check
>   the signs. If you're not here-
>   Welcome to the world of competitive
>   cheerleading. High school
>   divisions, please check the signs.
>   If you're not here-

Missy taking it all in.

> CHEER SQUAD #1
> Who art in Heaven, Hallowed be Thy
> name. Thy kingdom come, Thy will be
> done, on earth as it is in Heaven-

> CHEER SQUAD #2
> Broncos!

> CHEER SQUAD #3
> Ready? Okay!

At THE REGISTRATION AREA, Courtney and Whitney wait in line.
Suddenly, SOMEONE shoves Courtney. Furious, slamming her
duffel bag on the ground, she's ready to rumble.

> COURTNEY
> You cutter, I'm gonna kick your
> ass, you evil whore!

A six-year old TINY TOT CHEERLEADER stares up at Courtney. In
Junior All-Star garb, the tot smiles mischievously.

> TOT CHEERLEADER
> Get over it, hag!

The Tiny Tot Cheerleader stomps on Courtney's foot, punching
Courtney.

Whitney trying unsuccessfully to pull Courtney away as we --

INT. COMPETITION STAGE

ON STAGE...a PEEWEE ALL_STAR SQUAD performs.

A HIGH-STRUNG MOM runs up to the JUDGES PANEL, livid,
pointing at ONE JUDGE.

> HIGH-STRUNG MOM
> Hi. You, yes. Your head was down.
> Your head was down during that
> move. How are you gonna give a
> proper score if you're not looking,
> if your head is down during a move?

INT. BACKSTAGE/REGIONALS - DAY

BACKSTAGE, RCH enters. OTHER SQUADS wave and back-pat
relentlessly.

> DARCY
> Remember, they give extra points
> for alacrity and effulgence.

59.

                         KASEY
          Did we bring those?

                         DARCY
          Oh, no. Look who's here.

Striding in like confident sprinters, the CLOVERS enter.

                         KASEY
          Hi.

                         DARCY
          We're in trouble.

                         REGIONALS ANNOUNCER (O.S.)
          And now, making their first
          appearance at the U.C.A. California
          regionals, the East Compton
          Clovers!

                         CROWD
          Yeah, Clovers!

East Compton runs on to stage. Thumping MUSIC begins. They
explode into action.

The RCH SQUAD watch East Compton for the first time. Cocky
smiles are replaced by stupefied shock. Kasey gets swept
away, CHEERING. Darcy kicks her.

INT. PRESS AREA - MOMENTS LATER

Torrance and SQUAD interviewed by CHEER TV REPORTER.

                         CHEER TV REPORTER
          I'm standing here with five-time
          national returning champions, the
          Rancho Carne Toros. Leading the
          squad this year is senior Torrance
          Shipman. Torrance, one of the
          things we've come to expect from
          the Toros over the last few years
          is a highly original routine. Can
          we expect the same this year?

                         TORRANCE
          Well, I think everyone goes out
          there the same way, being as
          prepared as they can be and just
          hoping for the best. We're just
          glad to be back here... and eager
          to see what other squads have come
          up with.

A now-familiar AUDIO BITE comes over the loudspeakers.

> AUDIO BITE (O.S.)
> Prepare for total domination!
> Domination! Domination!

> COURTNEY
> Isn't that Sparky?

TOROS giving each other looks of concern.

> CHEER TV
> Thank you, Rancho Carne Toros, and
> good luck.

> TORRANCE
> (mumbles)
> Thanks.

> REGIONALS ANNOUNCER
> And now, the Mighty Muskrats of
> Mesa Cucamonga!

RCH SQUAD watching in jaw-dropping shock: It's the EXACT
routine.

> MISSY
> Spirit fingers.

> KASEY
> They stole our routine!

ANGLE ON: Bleachers - Aaron and Cliff both wave at Torrance.

ANGLE ON: Torrance waving back, horrified.

Aaron blows a kiss. Torrance blows one back. Cliff is
surprised but pleased.

> CHEER SQUAD #4 (O.S.)
> Pump! Pump! Pump it up!

Torrance yanking Missy aside.

> TORRANCE
> It's the curse.

> MISSY
> What?

> TORRANCE
> The Spirit Stick curse.

131

                    MISSY
Oh, God, will you lay off with
that? There's no curse, and you're
not going to Hades.

                 TORRANCE
News flash! Look around. We are in
Hades!

            EVENT COORDINATOR
Rancho Carne! You're up next!

INT. STAGE/REGIONALS - DAY

           REGIONALS ANNOUNCER
And now, from San Diego,
California, the five-time national
champions, the Rancho Carne Toros!

CROWD goes wild.

                JUDGE #1
I bet this is good.

SPARKY'S THEME begins... again. We see the exact same
routine.

                JUDGE #2
Didn't we just see this routine?

CLOVERS watching from backstage. Sharing an incredulous
TITTER.

ON STAGE Torrance and company yelling louder, smiling harder.

CROWD MEMBERS exchanging concerned looks. RCH finishes. BOOS
and POLITE APPLAUSE.

BIG RED on the sidelines - slamming her fist in frustration.

               BIG RED
What the eff -- ?

         REGIONALS ANNOUNCER (O.S.)
Ahem. The Rancho Carne Toros,
ladies and gentlemen.

                KASEY
           (almost crying)
Go, Toros!

                JUDGE #1
Think they screwed up.

TOROS exit. Torrance running into Isis and CLOVERS.

                    ISIS
          That was, um, interesting. Y'all
          should've just stuck with our
          routines.
                    (then)
          Don't worry. We'll send you a
          postcard from nationals.

INT. BACKSTAGE - CONTINUOUS

                    REGIONALS ANNOUNCER
          Next up, the Fighting Beavers of
          San Bernardino.

ACA OFFICIAL TAD FREEMAN pulls Torrance aside. Missy's
eavesdropping.

                    TAD FREEMAN
          Torrance Shipman?

                    TORRANCE
          Yes.

                    TAD FREEMAN
          Tad Freeman, Universal Cheer
          Association. We have a problem.

                    TORRANCE
          A problem?

                    TAD FREEMAN
          Oh, yes, a very big problem. I
          don't know if you can imagine...

Cliff locating Missy.

                    CLIFF
          Hey.

                    MISSY
          Hey.

                    TAD FREEMAN
          ...the incredible sense of deja vu
          I experienced as I was watching
          that last routine. It tends to make
          me suspicious-

Cliff trying to get Torrance's attention, Missy stops him.

>   MISSY
> I wouldn't just now.

>   CLIFF
> What?

>   MISSY
> Official cheer business.

>   CLIFF
> Come on. It's me.
>   (yelling)
> Hey, Torrance!

>   TAD FREEMAN
> You see, I-

Torrance shooing him away.

>   TORRANCE
>   (mouthing)
> Not now.

ANGLE ON: MISSY and CLIFF

>   MISSY
> That was smooth. Real smooth.

>   CLIFF
>   (shot down)
> I'll see her later.

>   MISSY
> All righty.

>   CLIFF
> Oh, uh, by the way, nice spirit
> fingers.

>   MISSY
>   (flipping a bird)
> Yeah. Well, here's another.

>   CLIFF
>   (putting it in his pocket)
> Thanks.

ANGLE ON: Torrance is on the grill.

>   TAD FREEMAN
> Obviously, your Toros aren't the
> only squad with this particular
> routine. Does the name Sparky
> Polastri mean anything to you?

                    TORRANCE
          Sparky Polastri?

                    TAD FREEMAN
          Mm-hmm. Apparently he's been
          peddling this same routine up and
          down the California coast. Six
          squads total. We're holding an
          emergency session of the
          discretionary panel.

                    TORRANCE
          About what?

                    TAD FREEMAN
          We've never had a situation like
          this before. We really should
          disqualify you and-

                    TORRANCE
          No, don't punish the squad. It was
          my choice to hire Sparky, not
          theirs. Don't penalize everyone for
          my bad judgment.

                    TAD FREEMAN
          But...since there's no precedent
          for this, there's nothing in the
          rule books that forbids it. It's
          simply frowned upon. And I suppose
          we can't disqualify you on those
          grounds alone. As defending
          champions, you are guaranteed a bid
          to Florida, but know that we'll be
          watching you. And don't expect to
          show up at finals with that
          routine.

Torrance is on the verge of tears, speechless.

BIG RED storming Torrance. Aaron in tow.

                    BIG RED
          What are you doing? You're wrecking
          everything I built!

                    AARON
          It's not totally her fault. I was
          the one that hooked her up -

                    BIG RED
          This season should have been gravy,
          okay? I handpicked the squad, I
          delivered an idiot-proof routine.

                    BIG RED (CONT'D)
                 (mimes putting something
                  on tray)
              Platter. Nationals. Hello?

Torrance is now spilling tears, looking ill.

                    TORRANCE
              Don't you mean a stolen routine?

                    BIG RED
              Oh. Don't be so naive, Torrance.
              Look, the truth is I was a real
              leader, okay? I did what I had to
              do to win at Nationals, and ever
              since I handed the reins over to
              you, you've run my squad into the
              ground! If I made any mistake as a
              squad leader, it wasn't borrowing
              cheers. It was announcing you as my
              successor.

Flustered, Torrance makes her exit.

                    AARON
                 (to Big Red)
              Uh-uh. Not cool. Hey, Tor. Tor.
              Wait, wait, wait, wait, wait.

Aaron catches Torrance.

                    TORRANCE
              Let me go. I just wanna get out of
              here.

                    AARON
              Hey, Big Red's a bitch. We all know
              that. Even she knows that.

                    TORRANCE
              I don't know what to do here,
              Aaron.

                    AARON
              Look. I know I haven't always been
              there for you since I went to
              college. It's been a rough
              transition, for both of us. But I
              still care about you as much as I
              ever did. You know that, right?

                    TORRANCE
              You do? Of course.

                    AARON
          Which is why I hate to see you like
          this, all stressed out. It's not
          good for you. You're a great
          cheerleader, Tor, and you're cute
          as hell. It's just that maybe...

Pulling Torrance in for a hug she doesn't want...

                    AARON (CONT'D)
          Maybe... you're just not captain
          material, and there's nothing wrong
          with that. Maybe you should
          consider letting Courtney and
          Whitney take over the squad.
          They're just like Big Red.

                    TORRANCE
          You want me to give up captain?

                    AARON
          Hey, let them deal with the
          politics. You just do what you do
          best, Tor. You cheer. Cheer, Tor.
          Okay? I just wanna see you happy.

EXT. SHIPMAN HOUSE - NIGHT

Aaron's Tracker pulling up. Torrance is fried.

                    TORRANCE
          Bye.

Kissing her enthusiastically, Aaron smiles. Torrance

                    AARON
          Sleep tight, sweetie.

Torrance exits, finding Cliff waiting outside her house. With
FLOWERS.

                    CLIFF
          Friend of yours?

                    TORRANCE
          He's my boyfriend.
              (distraught)
          Look, Cliff, I can explain.

                    CLIFF
          No. It's cool. Here, um, I made you
          a tape too.

Handing her the flowers and cassette, Cliff takes off.

> TORRANCE
>> Cliff --

INT. TORRANCE'S ROOM - NIGHT

On her bed holding the flowers, Torrance plays the cassette.

> CLIFF (V.O.)
>> Hey, Torrance, uh, it's me, Cliff.
>> Um, here's, uh- I wrote something,
>> uh, for you, so here it is.
>>> (singing)
>> Oh, Torrance / Can't stand your
>> cheerleading squad / But I love
>> your pom-pons / I'd feed you
>> bonbons all night. One, two, three,
>> four!

Bobbing her head to the beat it's lifting her mood --

> CLIFF (V.O.)
>> Yeah, you got me to feel all those
>> butterflies inside. / In your
>> locker I would hide / The truth /
>> It's only you I see / And you're
>> just what I need / I'd bring you
>> flowers everyday / Just to roll you
>> in the hay / Well, I'm feelin' fine
>> I'm right on time I know I'll get
>> my way.

-- Torrance jumping on the bed with her pom pons. Happy.

> CLIFF (V.O.)
>> And you're just what I need / And
>> you're just what I need / Not
>> everything works as it seems / Is
>> that so hard to believe? / 'Cause
>> you're just what I need / And
>> you're just what I need / Not
>> everything works as it seems / Is
>> that so hard to believe? / Shout!

INT. GYMNASIUM - DAY

Torrance striding into the gym. Whitney and Courtney flank,
walking her to the squad.

> COURTNEY
> Aaron called us last night. He told
> us you're turning the squad over to
> us.

> WHITNEY
> We want you to know that just
> because you bit the big one as
> captain, does not mean we're gonna
> be super hard on you.

> TORRANCE
> Oh.

> COURTNEY
> We'll treat you as if you didn't
> screw us into the ground.

> TORRANCE
> Gee, thanks.

> WHITNEY
> Everyone. Torrance is not to be
> harmed.

> COURTNEY
> We've already decided on a course
> of action. We're gonna forego
> nationals this year.

> WHITNEY
> Everyone's already agreed to it.

> MISSY
> Uh, except me.

> LES
> And me!

> COURTNEY
> Both of you can be replaced.

> TORRANCE
> I can't believe you guys. The only
> person who can officially resign
> the post of captain is the captain,
> and I'm not going anywhere.

> WHITNEY
> Then we'll have to overthrow you.

> COURTNEY
> Which we will!

> TORRANCE
> Enough! Our whole cheering career,
> we've staked our reputation on
> being the best, the most inventive.
> Now we finally have a chance to
> truly be original, and you're all
> running scared.

> COURTNEY
> She's crazy.

> TORRANCE
> I am not crazy, and I'm not
> resigning as captain either. You're
> gonna have to kill me first.

> WHITNEY
> That can be arranged.

> KASEY
> Shut it, Whitney! Let her talk!

> TORRANCE
> Look, I know I've screwed up
> royally as captain, but I believe
> in this squad, and I know we can
> bounce back from this. I'm not
> saying it's gonna be easy. It's
> gonna be hard work. We need a new
> routine, something amazing and
> fresh, and we've got less than
> three weeks till nationals. But if
> we can do it, if we can pull this
> off, then we can really call
> ourselves original. Now who's with
> me?

SQUAD cheers.

> SQUAD
> All right! Yeah. Yeah! Yeah!

> TORRANCE
>   (to Whit & Court)
> How 'bout it, girls? It's gonna be
> hard without you two.

> COURTNEY
> Fine.

> WHITNEY
> Sure. Whatever.

REBUILDING MONTAGE

En masse, they begin TRAINING as we cut to-

>   TORRANCE (V.O.)
>   Okay. Let's do this. We're gonna
>   devote every waking hour to
>   practice- before school, in between
>   classes and after school. Afternoon
>   practices will have to be twice as
>   long. We've gotta do whatever it
>   takes to be in perfect physical
>   shape.

EXT. RANCHO CARNE HIGH - DAY

Jan is on top of Missy, stretching her out.

>   MISSY
>   Yeah. You can go a little harder.
>   Yeah, that feels good.

>   FOOTBALL TIGHT END
>   Maybe we should join the squad.

>   SQUAD
>   Push. Oh, yeah.

>   RCH QUARTERBACK
>   Fag!

EXT. RANCHO CARNE FOOTBALL FIELD - NIGHT

>   TORRANCE (V.O.)
>   And since the football team sucks
>   no matter how hard we cheer, we'll
>   use night games to practice too.

INT. GYM - VARIOUS

A SNAPPY DANCE INSTRUCTION COUPLE demonstrate Lindy and
Jitterbug throws to Jan, Torrance, Missy and Lesley. Unusual,
cool, and they're getting it.

>   TORRANCE (V.O.)
>   But that's not all. We're gonna
>   study other types of movement, from
>   swing dance...

A BLUE UNITARD-CLAD INSTRUCTOR gesticulates to the squad, coaching them into an amazing Pilobolus-esque formation. The shit they're doing looks very cool. It's starting to work.

>   TORRANCE (V.O.)
>   ...to interpretive dance...

>   INTERPRETIVE DANCE INSTRUCTOR
>   ...you grow and you grow and you
>   bloom!

A MIME ARTIST is trapped in an invisible box.

>   TORRANCE (V.O.)
>   Even mime!

EXT. FIELD

SQUAD replicating MARTIAL ARTS moves, morphing fight moves into cheer choreography.

>   TORRANCE (V.O.)
>   We'll draw inspiration from martial
>   arts...

VIDEO MONTAGE of MUSICALS. Squad weeping sweat, but totally focused. It's clumsy, but improving.

>   TORRANCE (V.O.)
>   ...musicals, everything. You guys
>   know we've got the talent. We've
>   just gotta work our asses off and
>   trust our instincts. All of our
>   instincts.

EXT. DORM ROOM - DAY

Torrance knocks on a door. AARON opens it, then closes.

>   AARON
>   Tor! Wow! What are you doing here?

>   TORRANCE
>   Just wanted to come by and see you.
>   Is this a bad time?

>   AARON
>   Yeah. Yeah, yeah, yeah. I'm super
>   busy. I'm workin' on this project-

                    TORRANCE
          Yeah, you sound super busy. I guess
          that's it. You were too busy to
          believe in me.
               (reconsidering)
          Oh. No, no, but wait. You weren't
          too busy to sell me out to Courtney
          and Whitney, were you? Gee, now I'm
          confused. Well, I hope you're not
          too busy to hear this. Kiss my ass,
          Aaron! It's over!

With that she kicks the door open, revealing a LOVER wearing
a bra and panties, pulling up her pants. Torrance pats Aaron
on the shoulder.

                    TORRANCE (CONT'D)
          You're a great cheerleader, Aaron.
          It's just that... maybe you're not
          exactly boyfriend material. BUH-
          bye.

                    AARON'S LOVER
               (scoffs)
          You're a cheerleader?

Aaron slams the door as we cut to --

INT. GYM WEIGHT ROOM - DAWN

Torrance and various squad-mates weight-train. Missy bursts
in.

                    MISSY
          U.C.A. just posted the nationals
          list on the Internet. East Compton
          isn't on it. They couldn't raise
          the money in time. They're not
          going.

Torrance starts clanging weights onto the rack.

                    TORRANCE
          What do you mean, "They're not
          going"?

                    JAN
          Torrance, that's good news.

                    TORRANCE
          They cannot not go. That's not good
          news.

143

> JAN
> What are you talking about? They
> don't go, we win. Once again we're
> the best.

> TORRANCE
> I define best as competing against
> the best there is out there and
> beating them. They have to go.

INT. SHIPMAN HOUSE - DAY

Torrance is frantic. Dad, Mom, and Justin prepare breakfast.

> TORRANCE
> It's so unfair. The first inner-
> city squad to get a bid to
> Nationals, and they can't afford to
> go?

> JUSTIN
> Look, Mom. Her head is spinning off
> into another dimension.

> MRS. SHIPMAN
> Justin!

> MR. SHIPMAN
> The company gets hit up for money
> all the time, honey. I just can't.

> TORRANCE
> It's not that much money, Mr. Level-
> Playing-Field. Tell them the deal.
> Maybe they'll wanna help.

> MR. SHIPMAN
> Yeah? Okay, I'll make the call, but
> they'll probably say no.

> TORRANCE
> Don't let them. Think of how much
> it'll mean to East Compton. They
> deserve to go. Do the right thing,
> Dad!

Torrance books off to school. Mom and Dad's reaction
suggesting they like what he heard.

> MRS. SHIPMAN
> Did that just happen?

                    MR. SHIPMAN
          Yeah.

INT. EAST COMPTON HS GYMNASIUM - DAY

Five CLOVERS gather around Isis, brainstorming an essay.

                    ISIS
          Where we come from 'cheer' is not a
          word we hear very often --

                    LAVA
          They should call us 'inspiration
          leaders' instead.

                    JENELOPE
          Oh, that's deep. I like that.

                    LAFRED
          I don't know why we're writing to
          some talk-show host. It's like
          we're begging for charity.

                    ISIS
          It's not charity. Pauletta Patton's
          from our neighborhood. She'll
          understand why we need the money.

                    LAFRED
          Tell her we need to buy donuts. Her
          big butt will understand that.

                    JENELOPE
          Ha-ha! Stop being
          counterproductive, all right?

                    LAFRED
          Lava, please stop teaching her
          these big words before she chokes
          on one.

                    JENELOPE
          No, better I choke you, Lafred.

                    LAFRED
          Look, Jenelope -

                    ISIS
          You guys, stop! Please. Damn!

                    LAFRED
          Well, tell her about the late-night
          practices we've been having.

                    ISIS
        There you go. That's the kind of
        stuff she wants to hear about.

                    LAVA
        Now, we're talking.

Torrance walking tentatively into Clover territory. Holding a
check, she approaches Isis.

                    TORRANCE
        You guys have to go to Nationals.

                    ISIS
        Did you come up here just to tell
        me that?

                    TORRANCE
            (handing her a check)
        Here. I got my dad's company to
        sponsor you guys.

                    ISIS
        What is this, hush money?

                    TORRANCE
        No.

                    ISIS
        Oh, right. It's guilt money. You
        pay our way in and you sleep better
        at night knowing how your whole
        world is based on one big, old fat
        lie. Well, you know what?

Isis rips the check up and lets the pieces fall to the floor.

                    ISIS (CONT'D)
        We don't need you.

                    TORRANCE
        Why do you have to be so mean? I'm
        just trying to do the right thing
        here.

                    ISIS
        I'm trying to be strong for my
        squad, okay? That's what a captain
        does.

                    TORRANCE
        Well, I'm a captain too, you know.
        And I'm trying to make it right.

                    ISIS
          You wanna make it right? Then when
          you go to Nationals? Bring it.
          Don't slack off because you feel
          sorry for us. That way, when we
          beat you, we'll know it's because
          we're better.

                    TORRANCE
          I'll bring it. Don't worry.

                    ISIS
          I never do.

EXT. RCH HALLWAY - DAY

Torrance handing out permission slips to Jan, Les, and
Courtney.

Tor lights up when she spots Cliff walking towards the
cafeteria. Cliff is lost in the music of his headset. She
taps him on the shoulder to get his attention.

                    TORRANCE
          I listened to your tape. I loved
          it.

                    CLIFF
          Great.

                    TORRANCE
          Can I talk to you? I was upset that
          night. Aaron gave me a ride home.
          It was just a good-night kiss. It
          meant nothing.

                    CLIFF
          Oh. I'm sorry.

                    TORRANCE
          And I wanted you to know that I
          broke up with him.

                    CLIFF
               (fake enthusiasm)
          Congratulations.

                    TORRANCE
          He didn't believe in me. You did!

                    CLIFF
          Whatever.

Cliff walking away, putting his headset back on.

                  TORRANCE
           (yelling after him)
       That's important to me! You
       believed in me!

STUDENTS freeze to stare at Torrance's plea.

INT. PANTONE LIVING ROOM - DAY

Cliff catching Missy marking the new routine. Mocking her.

                  MISSY
       Bite me.

                  CLIFF
       Hanging out with the airheads has
       really sharpened your verbal
       skills, huh?

                  MISSY
       Screw you.

                  CLIFF
       Said the cheerleader.

                  MISSY
       That's right, I am a cheerleader,
       and you're a dumb ass. Torrance
       likes you, okay? She likes you.

                  CLIFF
       She has an odd way of showing it.

                  MISSY
       Don't be stupid. She broke up with
       her boyfriend for you.

                  CLIFF
       Yeah.

                  MISSY
       Look. Do us all a favor and get
       over yourself and tell her how you
       feel.

                  CLIFF
       I thought I had.

> MISSY
> Well, try again. And let me give
> you a little tip from a
> cheerleader. Be aggressive. B-E
> aggressive.

INT. STUDIO/CLOVERS GYMNASIUM - BACK AND FORTH

> ANNOUNCER (O.S.)
> Now back to Pauletta!

PAULETTA CHYRON flying through frame revealing a TALK SHOW
host PAULETTA PATTON center stage.

> PAULETTA
> Thank you. Thank you. Today on
> Pauletta, it's "Wish Day"!

BACK IN THE GYM, the CLOVERS nervously smiling for a CAMERA.

> PAULETTA (CONT'D)
> (applause)
> Today's letter comes from East
> Compton, California.
> "Dear Pauletta: Where we come
> from... cheer is not a word that
> you hear very often, but that's
> what we are, the cheerleaders of
> East Compton High School. They
> should really call us inspiration
> leaders, because that's what we do.
> We inspire the people from our
> neighborhoods to believe that our
> team can win. That's why we're
> asking you to fulfill our wish to
> send us to the national
> cheerleading competition for the
> first time." Well, Clovers, you got
> your wish. Audience, the East
> Compton Clovers!

PAULETTA LOGO splitting, revealing CLOVERS ONSCREEN.

ON ISIS excitedly holding the mic as SQUAD is thrilled.

> ISIS
> Hi, Pauletta. We just wanna say how
> thankful we are for all of your
> help.

> JENELOPE
> Pauletta, you my girl! You the
> bomb, baby!

> LAFRED
> Ooh, Pauletta, girl, we love you so
> much. You don't have to lose a
> pound. We love you just the way you
> are!

> ISIS
> We're gonna make you an honorary
> Clover for life. Thank you so much.

PRODUCER handing Pauletta a CLOVERS UNIFORM.

> PAULETTA
> I'm gonna look good in this, y'all.

EXT. ALL-STAR SPORTS RESORT

SIGNAGE reads 'WELCOME CHEERLEADERS, YOU'RE ALL WINNERS!'

CHYRON: UNIVERSAL CHEER ASSOCIATION NATIONALS, DAYTONA,
FLORIDA

INT. CHAMPIONSHIP ORIENTATION/WELCOME TENT

SPONSORS TABLE HOSTS pass out GOODIE BAGS.HOSTS &
HOSTESSESS do orientation SPIELS in quick-cut succession.
CHAMPIONSHIP MERCHANDISE selling like hotcakes, a CASH-
REGISTER SYMPHONY.

Torrance and Missy walking arm in arm through SWARMS of
COMPETITORS.

> TORRANCE
> So, is your family coming?

> MISSY
> I don't know if Cliff's coming.

> TORRANCE
> I totally blew it with Cliff.

> MISSY
> Forget it. My brother's an idiot.

> TORRANCE
> You're his sister. You don't see
> him like I do.

> MISSY
> Yeah, and that's a good thing,
> 'cause that would be a crime.

COMPETITORS everywhere as they head inside.

                    JAN
          Hey, ladies, wanna see my Spirit
          Stick?

INT. SPORTS RESORT/HOTEL - NIGHT

Torrance pacing nervously with the phone.

INT. CLIFF'S ROOM - NIGHT

                    CLIFF (V.O.)
          Hey, this is Cliff. Leave a message
          after the-

Torrance hanging up, just as Cliff dives for the phone.

                    CLIFF
          Hello. Hello?

EXT. INDIANA JONES THEATER - DAY - ESTABLISHING

CELEBRATORY CHATTER of CROWD entering the theatre.

                    NATIONALS ANNOUNCER (V.O.)
          Lock your door. Bolt your windows.
          Daytona, Florida, has been invaded
          by teenage cheerleaders. And what
          do they want?

T-shirt #1: *CHEERLEADING IS LIFE!* T-shirt #2: *We're not
cocky, just the best!*; T-shirt #3: *Another year, another trip
to nationals!*

                    NATIONALS ANNOUNCER (V.O.)
          The chance to be the number one
          cheerleading squad in the country.
          You know, in high school, couldn't
          pay a cheerleader to talk to me.
          Now, I'm surrounded by 'em!

*Germantown Cheerleading -- it's a Germantown thing, you
wouldn't understand; USC gamecocks! Our cocks are up and
coming!; Give me Moorehead, or give me death.*

                    NATIONALS ANNOUNCER
          And let's face it, any sport that
          combines gymnastics, dance and
          short skirts is okay by me.
                    (MORE)

>   NATIONALS ANNOUNCER (CONT'D)
>   ESPN 2 welcomes you to sunny
>   Daytona, Florida, for the Universal
>   Cheer Association Nationals 2000.
>   Fifty squads from fifty high
>   schools across the nation... are
>   gathered here to duke it out. You
>   wanna talk pressure? Ha-ha. These
>   kids are feelin 'it. One individual
>   mistake can cost a squad
>   everything. Who's got spirit? We
>   do, baby. Only on the Deuce.

INT. INDIANA JONES THEATER - CONTINUOUS

AT THE STAGE ENTRANCE, the SQUADS are preparing backstage, stretching.

CLOVERS are prepping. Torrance approaches tentatively, pulling Isis aside.

>   TORRANCE
>   Hey. Watch going out of bounds.
>   They deduct like crazy for that
>   stuff.

>   ISIS
>   You going for sainthood or
>   somethin'?

>   TORRANCE
>   You don't wanna blow it on
>   something tiny.

>   ISIS
>   Look, me and my squad made it to
>   the big show without any of your
>   help. I think we can handle it.

Isis turns, rallying her troops.

>   ISIS (CONT'D)
>   Stay in bounds! If any of you step
>   outside that ugly blue carpet, you
>   are dead.
>   (to Torrance)
>   Happy?

>   TORRANCE
>   Yes.

                    ISIS
              (re: Kasey)
          Tell your girl on the end she's
          about a half second early on all
          her moves.

                    TORRANCE
          Okay, I will. Happy?

                    ISIS
          Yep. Hey, remember. Bring it.

                    JENELOPE
          And what the hell was that about?

                    ISIS
          We just understand each other,
          that's all.

Isis catching Torrance directing Kasey.

                    ISIS (CONT'D)
          All right, let's do this. One, two,
          three. Clovers!

EXT. INDIANA JONES THEATER - DAY

ENTRYWAY PLACARDS read: PRELIMINARIES

MONTAGE: SQUADS performing; JUDGES scoring; CHEERLEADERS
FALLING; Hugging. Crying. Cheering.

ON EMCEE:

                    EMCEE #1
          The field has been narrowed, and
          the advancing squads will move on
          to tomorrow's finals. Defending
          champs, the Toros, have managed to
          come back from a humiliating
          showing at Regionals. But the real
          Cinderella story here, of course,
          is the Clovers of East Compton,
          California.

INT. SPORTS RESORT - ROOM - NIGHT

TOROS sprawled out slumber-party style. Kasey's popping zits.

                    COURTNEY
          Kasey's popping zits again.

83.

                         DARCY
               Gross, Kasey. You're totally
               bedaubing the mirror. Clean it off.

                         KASEY
               Okay, okay!

                         MISSY
               I don't know what's scarier,
               neurotic cheerleaders or the
               pressure to win. I could make a
               killing selling something like Diet
               Prozac.

                         TORRANCE
               Thank God you're here this season,
               Missy. I couldn't have done it
               alone.

                         MISSY
                    (faux cry)
               Oh. Tear.

                         TORRANCE
               No, I mean it!

O.S. SQUADS PRACTICING in the dark. Missy goes to her
balcony.

                         MISSY
                    (yelling)
               Shut up! You don't have it yet, you
               don't have it! Give it up already!

EXT. INDIANA JONES THEATER - DAY - ESTABLISHING

ENTRYWAY PLACARDS read: FINALS

TV CAMERAS and VARIOUS CREW ready the venue as SPECTATORS
trickle in.

                         NATIONALS ANNOUNCER (V.O.)
               Daytona, Florida, day number two.
               By sundown, only one squad... can
               call themselves U.C.A. National
               Champions 2000.

INT. BACKSTAGE - CONTINUOUS

Courtney slamming her duffle to the ground.

              COURTNEY
Shit! Where the hell are my spanky
pants?

            RANDOM GIRL
What's that on his head?

Justin running around. With SPANKIES on his head.

              JUSTIN
Don't be shy, ladies. Donations are
always welcome.
      (to Missy)
Hey, babe. Are you in a giving
mood?

              MISSY
Sure.

Yanking spankies off and smacking him on the head.

              JUSTIN
Aah!

            TORRANCE
Get lost, freak, or I'm gonna tell
your friends that you were at a
cheerleading competition.

              JUSTIN
You wouldn't.

            TORRANCE
Oh, I would.

               JAN
Hey, I recognize these.

ANOTHER AREA

ANGLE ON: TWO COMPETITORS doing some post-game.

          RANDOM GIRL #2
That was perfect. Your basket toss
was amazing, and no one saw that
landing.

Pulling her hands away from her mouth, TOOTHLESS GIRL is
covered in blood.

          TOOTHLESS GIRL
Really?

                    RANDOM GIRL #2
          We should find your tooth.

IN ANOTHER AREA

ON LES, waiting backstage, greeting fellow competitor TIM.

                    LES
               Hey. That last lift you did was
               amazing.

                    TIM
               Thanks. Hey, good luck out there.

                    LES
               Thanks, man. I'm Les.

                    TIM
               I'm - I'm Tim.

                    LES
               Nice to meet you.

                    TIM
               Hey, I'll, uh, see you around?

                    LES
               Yeah.

Les exhaling the butterflies.

ANOTHER AREA BACKSTAGE

As a COACH is calming a NERVOUS GIRL.

                    COACH #1
               Okay, now focus and don't be
               nervous.

                    NERVOUS GIRL
               I'm not nervous.

                    COACH #1
               No, just try not to think about the
               stakes, okay?

                    NERVOUS GIRL
               I'm totally cool. I'm so ready.

                    COACH #1
               The main thing that you must
               remember is always smile!

A PROJECTILE of PUKE firehoses onto the coach.

KASEY and DARCY clocking this, tossing their power bars out
in disgust.

                    NERVOUS GIRL
          Sorry.

ANOTHER AREA BACKSTAGE, Clovers prepping to go on, nervous.

                    ISIS
          You guys, look. Gather up. Guys, we
          got this. We have done this routine
          a million times. Just relax. Forget
          about all those faces out there and
          just imagine that we're back at our
          school, in our gym just doin' our
          thing. We'll be fine.

                    NATIONALS COORDINATOR (O.S.)
          East Compton Clovers, you're up!

                    ISIS
          All right, now let's do this,
          Clovers.

                    SQUAD
          Yeah! Raise the ceiling! One, two,
          three! You know!

                    EMCEE (O.S.)
          Ladies and gentlemen, please
          welcome from East Compton,
          California, the Clovers!

The Clovers RUN ONSTAGE to SLAMMING MUSIC. They build and
dismantle pyramids, stunts and inventive sequences with
staggering originality. The earth moves...from their
creativity, risk, and personality.

There's no idling, just pedal-to-metal choreography. Complete
with dangerous stunts and crowd-pleasing spectacle.

CAPACITY CROWD eating it up.

BACKSTAGE TOROS watching from the sidelines. Torrance
clenching her jaw. Missy digging her nails into her arms.

JUDGES burning pencil on paper, racking up points for the
Clovers.

CENTER STAGE CLOVERS moving and shaking their hearts out.

                    EMCEE (O.S.) (CONT'D)
          Let's hear it for the East Compton
          Clovers!

BACKSTAGE Missy pointing to the bleachers.

IN THE STANDS: reveal CLIFF. Waving to Torrance and Missy. Torrance beaming with excitement, instantly revived.

EXT. BACKSTAGE

> TORRANCE
> Okay, guys, let's go out there and
> do our best. Nothing hits the
> floor. We stick it. Hands in.

> LES
> Trust on three. One, two, three.

> SQUAD
> Trust! Go, Toros! Yeah!

EXT. CENTER STAGE

TOROS positioning, backs to audience, heads down. Drama.

> NATIONALS ANNOUNCER
> Welcome the five-time... national
> champions from San Diego,
> California..

> AUDIENCE
> Go, Toros! Yeah!

> NATIONALS ANNOUNCER (V.O.)
> ...the Rancho Carne Toros!

> SQUAD/AUDIENCE
> Yea! Go, Toros! Let's go! Go,
> Toros! All right! Yeah! Yeah! Oh!
> - Toros! Yeah!

EXT. CENTER STAGE

All the pieces come together like a live-action video-game, complete with SFX: karate chops, forties-syle swing and jitterbug moves, some disco parody and Pilobolus builds. Pretty spectacular. It's witty, creative, and totally fresh.

IN THE BLEACHERS, CARVER rocking out with her crutches.

Tor's PARENTS Bruce and Christine Shipman rocking with joy and pride, Justin not so sure.

ON CLIFF rocking along.

THE CLOVERS watch from the side, impressed, very worried.

ONSTAGE: TOROS go for the ground-up Wolf's Wall.

TORRANCE locks the stunt. Elated to be at the top and sticking it!

THE AUDIENCE GASPS with acknowledgement of the difficulty ECHOING through the venue. THE SQUAD nails it.

ISIS' jaw drops. A begrudging shake of the head, she leads the APPLAUSE. THE CROWD loves it!

EVEN JUSTIN gives it up in his CHEERLEADING = DEATH t-shirt.

THE JUDGES move their pencils.

BACKSTAGE TOROS yelping, whooping, and hugging with collective relief.

> NATIONALS ANNOUNCER
> Let's hear it for the defending
> Champions, the Rancho Carne Toros!

EXT. CENTER STAGE

A PRODUCTION PERSON coaxes the TEN FINALIST SQUADS into a semi-circle around the TROPHY TABLE. Hyperventilation mixed with WEEPING, WHIMPERING, doubled-over panic and misguided attempts to appear calm is the general vibe.

> EMCEE #1
> Ladies and gentlemen, our five
> finalist teams have taken the
> stage, so please give a warm
> welcome to our emcees, editor of
> Cheer Fashion magazine, Ms. Brandi
> Tattersol, and U.C.A. president,
> Mr. Johnny Garrison.

The EMCEE takes Center Stage with BRANDI TATTERSOL, and JOHNNY GARRISON.

> JOHNNY GARRISON
> And now, ladies and gentlemen, the
> moment you've all been waiting for,
> the award ceremony for U.C.A. 2000.
> Five finalist squads, and only one
> will walk away with the grand prize
> trophy and the check for
> $20,000.00.
>   (MORE)

159

> JOHNNY GARRISON (CONT'D)
> And so, in third place, from New
> Pope High School in New Pope,
> Mississippi, the New Pope
> Cavaliers! Let's hear it for 'em.
> Well done, ladies. And now, Brandi,
> would you do the honors?

> BRANDI
> And in second place - and this was
> a tough decision, as there were two
> outstanding performances this year.
> In second place, from San Diego,
> California, the Rancho Carne Toros!

Torrance is in shock. Courtney GASPS.

> COURTNEY
> Second place? Hell, yeah!

Missy and Torrance celebrated, collecting the 2ND PLACE
TROPHY.

> NATIONALS ANNOUNCER
> And now, the winners, of this
> year's National High School
> Cheerleading Championships, the
> East Compton Clovers of East
> Compton, California!
> Congratulations, Clovers. Let's
> hear it!

The CLOVERS are stupefied. Jumping up and down and screaming
and shrieking with unadulterated joy. Lava and Isis get on
LaFred and Jovan's shoulders, and share the job of holding
and lifting the FOUR FOOT HIGH TROPHY over the MASSES.

> CLOVERS
> Yeah! - We did it! We did it!

> ISIS
> Number one! Yeah!

CLOVERS posing with their GIANT check.

> EMCEE #1
> Ladies and gentlemen, let's hear it
> out there! Let's hear it for all of
> our squads!

Isis and Torrance grabbing a moment.

> ISIS
> Torrance.

                    TORRANCE
          Whoa, nice check.

                    ISIS
          I just want to say, captain to
          captain, I respect what you guys
          did out there. You guys were good.

                    TORRANCE
          Thanks. You were better.

                    ISIS
          We were, huh?

Laughing, they go back to their squads.

ON MISSY waving a SPIRIT STICK.

                    MISSY
          Look, my very own Spirit Stick. So,
          you think the curse is broken?

                    TORRANCE
          I don't believe in curses anymore.

                    MISSY
          Oh, really?

                    TORRANCE
          No.

Missy dropping the SPIRIT STICK the ground. Torrance
hesitates - wanting to grab for it - but lets it fall.

                    TORRANCE (CONT'D)
               (picking it up)
          Well, maybe we should burn that,
          just in case.

                    MISSY
          Right!

LAUGHING, they bear hug, as Cliff's joining them.

                    CLIFF
          Congratulations.

                    MISSY
               (hugging)
          Oh, thanks. Uh, you remember my
          friend Torrance, right?

                    CLIFF
          Yeah, I think so.

                    MISSY
          We'll talk later. Les!

                    CLIFF
          So, second place? How's it feel?

                    TORRANCE
          Feels like first.

Torrance pulls Cliff in for a big kiss. Everybody's watching.
Doesn't stop 'em.

THE END.

TOROS and CLOVERS and CAST enjoying a CURTAIN CALL and gag
reel to HEY MICKEY.

PEYTON REED:

Jessica, I mean, I remember even at the time as a white guy making a cheerleader movie that dealt with issues of race is so fraught. And it's kind of a microcosm for America now. It's very hard. I mean, I don't know if you've read "White Fragility" or seen the lecture on it, but like the idea of like white people knowing how to talk about race. Yeah, yeah. An issue of just like guilt or shame...

JESS:

Yeah. All of the above. You know, the WGA prohibits members from talking about uncredited production rewrites. But it's very common in the business. We all do it. There's no shame in it. It's a reality of the business. And it's like oftentimes I think of writers, we're like trying to give the best pass to the actors so they can make the three-point shot. Production is a team sport, and when you're doing punch-up, when the actor feels comfortable, the difference is palpable.

You build the house, you do the blueprint, and then the furniture is going to move around a little bit, you know? And so there are some great pieces of furniture that move here and there.

But I'm very proud of the movie.

https://www.wga.org/

ANNOTATIONS

CONTENT IS QUEEN, BUT CONTEXT IS GOD.

To really understand the final content, you have to understand the original context. In that spirit, I'm including the following annotations and deleted scenes for a couple reasons:

1) So you can see that screenwriting is a process and a journey.

2) So you can see how campy and over-the-top the early drafts were. As a young writer in search of tone, much of my dialogue was inspired by the banter of gay men in general and the hyperbole of drag queens, specifically. Big shout out to the legendary performance artist Vaginal Davis, whose punk-drag energy inspired some of the early explorations around the Clovers.

3) Now that you can see what was in the original DNA of the material and how that evolved, it might be helpful to understand my intention. So while this influence gives scenes that "pushed" feeling, sometimes the heightened camp aesthetics might easily be misconstrued as cartoony. It's a tone zone and when you're striking a balance, you find that balance via exploration. These dynamics were useful even though subsequently pared down and pulled back. You can see their influence remains most notably in Sparky Polastri and the Courtney/Whitney drama.

Who's Trisha?

CHEERFEVER

By
Jessica Bendinger

Please enjoy my weird quasi-ransom style collage. If this doesn't establish tone, I don't know what does.

I am sure I was delighted to find an "S" for Torrance's last name…Shipman. A neighbor in Weho had that last name and I was like, Done! Sold!

I also felt like Torrance was conceived in Torrance - it just felt like a hilariously SoCal name.

Who is Debby? And where did I get these? This is pre-Clip Art, people.

6/13/97

I do know Marcy.

1   OPENING CREDITS: 1

> Nice repetition. Do not copy me.

A FILM-STRIP FRAME scrolls shakily into frame accompanied by
a flat TONE. A 1950'S STYLE FONT reads: *The History of
Cheerleading*

> In case you missed it, apparently I was going for "tone."

TONE. An IMAGE of RUDY VALLEE, with fur coat and megaphone.
TONE. FLAPPER CHEERLEADERS. TONE. 1940's, 1950's CHEERLEADERS
with long, poodle skirts. The TONE becomes the sound of a
RAVE WHISTLE BLOWING.

TO THUMPING TECHNO, an ARRAY OF SQUADS do it all. Breakneck
MONTAGE of the basic food-groups in modern-day championship
cheerleading: Championship-style ARMS (BLADES; DAGGERS; V'S;
LUNGES); JUMPS (TOE-TOUCHES, PIKES, HURDLERS; AND HERKIES);
DANCE MOTIONS (SHIMMIES; DROPS; THRUSTS; PUNCHES);
STUNTS/LIFTS/TOSSES/PYRAMIDS; SIGNAGE, CROWD-LEADING moments.

> It's called research, y'all.

The RAVE WHISTLE becomes the sound of a REFEREE WHISTLE as we

                                              DISSOLVE TO:

2   INT. SPORTS ARENA   2

A CO-ED HIGH-SCHOOL CHEERLEADING SQUAD performs center-court.

> I still think Titans is funnier than Toros, and less confusing, because the lead character's name is Torrance. Sorry, Peyton. #facts

                         SQUAD
            We are the Titans! The Mighty Titans! We're
            so Titanic, we must be Titans!

TORRANCE SHIPMAN, a vivacious, blonde 17 year-old with
Pebbles Flintstone hair, commands the floor. Oh, instead of
high school letters, *USA* in chenille stretches across each
chest/sweater.

TORRANCE touches her Minnie Mouse bangs and smacks her
blue-glitter lipgloss, adjusting her SPANKY-PANTS. The
bottoms feature: the OLYMPIC RING INSIGNIA in varsity-style
block chenille lettering. On second glance, every pair of
bloomers shares this touch.

> I love this. I'm proud of this. I stan this.

> Update: Peyton says legal couldn't clear "Titans."

                         TORRANCE
            Achoo!

                         SQUAD
            Bless you!

In the background, A BANNER with OLYMPIC RINGS waves mildly
in the arena air.

                   GIRL SQUAD MEMBERS
                  (4/4 time, chanting)
            I'm sexy. I'm cute. I'm pop-u-lar to boot.
            I'm bitchin. Great hair. The boys all like

> If you're confused, don't be. The screenplay originally opened at the Olympics. I'm a genius. I still stan this.

6/13/97   p.2

                    GIRL SQUAD MEMBERS (cont'd)
    to stare. I'm wanted. I'm hot. I'm
    everything you're not. I'm pretty. I'm
    cool. I dominate the school. Who am I?
    Just guess. Guys wanna touch my chest. I'm
    rockin. I smile. And many think I'm vile!
    I'm flying. I jump. You can look, but
    don't you hump! I'm major. I roar. I swear,
    I'm not a whore! We cheer and, we lead. We
    act like we're on speed! Hate us cause we're
    beautiful? Well, we don't like you either,
    we're cheerleaders! We are cheerleaders!

> Still perfect. You're welcome.

EACH FEMALE CHEERLEADER springs into frame via JUMP or STUNT.

                    TORRANCE
        I'm Tu-tu-Torrance!

Like a BAD 1970'S SHOW-OPEN, we FREEZE on Torrance in
mid-air, her face contorted into a shriek, doin' a Herkie.
The word TORRANCE in VARSITY BLOCK LETTERING wipes over her
frozen image. It's 'Trainspotting' and 'The Love Boat' all at
once! At a hyper-fast clip, each cheerleader suffers the
same ignominious treatment.

> Did I mention "tone"? In all seriousness, I'm probably overdoing it. However, that's the idea.

An Asian beauty with peroxide blonde hair, WHITNEY DOW, 16,
is tan, tan, tan.

                    WHITNEY
        I'm Wu-Wu-Whitney! (freeze on Hi-C jump)

> Side note: Whitney Dow is one of my best guy friends. His daughters love this.

Icy Breck-Girl blonde, COURTNEY EGBERT, 16, flips between
bitchy passivity and bitchy impertinence. Nightmare.

                    COURTNEY
        Cu-Cu-Cu-Courtney! (freeze on X-out)

> Breck Girls were the equivalent of Cover Girls. See Kim Basinger.

Jet-black Lulu bob and movie-star attitude, DARCY ESTRADA is
a rich, 17-year-old know-it-all. Stacked.

                    DARCY
        Dude, it's Da-Darcy! (freeze on double nine
        jump)

Hello, horsey girl. CARVER RIZCHEK is a 16-year-old rep for
Thighs-R-Us.

> This is complicated in 2020. I'm using the language of objectification, and I don't think I would do that now tbh.

                    CARVER
        I'm big, bad Carver! (freeze on lib heel
        stretch)

15-year-old KASEY is a scrawny mess whose braces are about to
blind you --

> First of all, Carver is named after Larry Karaszewski's daughter. Secondly, I was trying to represent a variety of body types in a non-shaming way. I don't know that I succeeded.

                              KASEY
                Just call me Kasey! (freeze on scorpion)

BIG RED, an over-developed 18 with red ringlets and a black
heart, takes center stage.

> This still makes me laugh.

                              BIG RED
                Call me Big Red!

                            TORRANCE
                And I'm still Torrance!

The MALE SQUAD MEMBERS appear in profile next to the
aforementioned gals, a seemingly endless line of cheerleaders.

> Can't believe this didn't make the movie. It's awesome.

Like an ESTHER WILLIAMS/MICKEY MOUSE CLUB sequence, the GUYS
YELL, wave and pop in and out of frame at FORTY-FIVE DEGREE
ANGLES: JAN! LESLEY! BROOKE! KELLY! PAT! SANDY! TERRY!

Finishing the chant, the girls move into pre-toe-touch-jump
position. Torrance smiles broadly before lift-off. Pushing
off the floor in slo mo - Torrance's face morphs from glee to
panic, her mouth becoming a scream. A real SCREAM...of
terror.

THE CROWD gasps collectively, some MALE CROWD MEMBERS smiling
and high-fiving each other.

A PANEL OF OLYMPIC JUDGES scribble sternly on scoresheets.   Again, lol.

> I like how PG I'm trying to be. Obviously, in Australia, "fanny" might be an R-rating. This is likely obvious to no one, except Australians and me.

TORRANCE'S HANDS try to cover her exposed FANNY. Her spanky
pants have disappeared, and there's nothing but <u>butt</u>.

THE JUDGES burn pencil. The sound of A BUZZER melds with
Torrance's WIDE-MOUTHED SCREAM as the JUDGES raise their
SCORECARDS. The camera zooms into Torrance's UVULA, her
SCREAMING mixing with the sound of an ALARM CLOCK
bbbrrrringing as we

> This is pretty damn close.

INT. DORM ROOM - MORNING   3

Two bunk-beds, FOUR SLEEPING GALS. Torrance bolts upright in
bed, clutching her pigtails and still SCREAMING bloody murder.

                            TORRANCE
                Nine point two?!?!!!!!!! Bronze? Bronze my
                ass!   Aaaarrgh!!!

Whitney, Courtney and Big Red jolt awake, irritated.

But Torrance cannot stop, as the camera zooms back into her
gaping yap, becoming the screams of HUNDREDS OF TEENS as we

CHEER FEVER

By

Jessica Bendinger

JUNE 9, 1999
FINAL WHITE

1   OVER THE UNIVERSAL LOGO   1

we hear a tinny-sounding AUDIO COLLAGE of old-school, 50's-
style cheerleading squads.

> OLD-SCHOOL CHEERLEADERS (O.S.)
> Rah rah, sis boom bah! Hip hurray
> and cha cha cha!

2   FADE UP ON BLACK AND WHITE FOOTAGE: 2

A series of SLOW-MOTION IMAGES of classic, whitebread-
Americana cheerleaders cheering their hearts out.

> OLD-SCHOOL CHEERLEADERS (O.S.)
> Push 'em back, push 'em back,
> waaay back!

(Glad that was cut.)

Over the montage, a TITLE appears in bright varsity-style
chenille lettering:

Cheer fever

After a moment, the tinny audio starts to DISSOLVE into a
deep pulsin' 4/4 BEAT. Getting louder. And louder.

Until, with a jarring RIP, the image TEARS OPEN to reveal...

3   INT. HIGH SCHOOL GYMNASIUM - NIGHT   3

Full color. The camera ROCKETS downward, straight at A CO-ED
HIGH-SCHOOL CHEERLEADING SQUAD who performs at center-court.

(One last hurrah for the Titans. This joke is better. I stand by that.)

> SQUAD
> We are the Titans! The Mighty
> Titans! We're so Titanic, we must
> be Titans!

This is not your mother's cheerleading squad!

BIG RED, a sexy, over-developed 18-year-old with red ringlets
and a black heart, commands the floor. **FDS** in chenille
s-t-r-e-t-c-h-e-s across her sweater.

TORRANCE SHIPMAN, a vivacious, blonde 17 year-old with
Pebbles Flintstone hair, commands the floor. **USA** in chenille
stretches across her sweater.

(One last OLYMPICS hangnail from earlier draft. May she rest in peace.)

The squad's SPANKY PANTS feature the TBD FILIAS DEUS LOGO
proudly emblazoned across each butt cheek.

In the background, a BANNER reading 'FILIAS DEUS TITANS"
waves mildly in the gymansium air. The ladies shake it in a
balls-out sexy amazing dance thing.

                    KASEY
          Just call me Kasey!

Big Red takes up center position once again.

                    BIG RED
          I'm still Big Red.

With that, the squad STOPS in their tracks and collectively
points toward Big Red, who <u>really</u> starts to gyrate.

                    BIG RED
               (continuing; in 4/4
                time)
          I sizzle. I scorch. But now I
          pass the torch. The ballots are
          in, and one girl had to win.
          She's perky, she's fun, and now
          she's number one! K-k-kick it,
          Torrance! Tu-tu-tu-Torrance!

Big Red exits just as...

TORRANCE SHIPMAN, a vivacious, blonde 17-year-old with
Pebbles Flintstone hair, is thrust into the limelight.

                    TORRANCE
          I'm strong and/ I'm loud! I'm
          gonna make you proud! I'm Tu-tu-
          Torrance! Your captain, Torrance!
          Let's...go...Titans!

5   On command, the girls begin in a sexy, synchronized series   5
     of moves, finally landing in a pre-toe-touch-jump position.

     Torrance smiles broadly before lift-off. Pushing off the
     floor in SLO-MO, her face morphs from glee to panic, her
     mouth becoming a scream. A <u>real</u> scream...of TERROR.

6   The STUDENT BODY CROWD gasps collectively, some MALE   6
     CROWD MEMBERS smiling and high-fiving each other.

7   TORRANCE'S HANDS try to cover her exposed FANNY. Her   7
     spanky pants have disappeared, and there's nothing but
     <u>BUTT</u>.

8   The camera ZOOMS into Torrance's UVULA, her SCREAMING   8
     mixing with the sound of an ALARM CLOCK rrringing as we...

9   INT. TORRANCE'S ROOM - MORNING   9

Torrance bolts upright in bed, clutching her pigtails and
still SCREAMING bloody murder.

                                        SMASH CUT TO:

                    TORRANCE
          Aaaaaaaaa!!!
               (catching her breath)
          Holy shit.

10   EXT. SHIPMAN HOUSE - DAY   10

Honking is AARON GILBERT, 18, a great-looking dude: tan,
muscular and not a hair out of place. He pulls curbside in
his Geo Tracker, loaded down with guy crap for college.

MR. AND MRS. SHIPMAN, both mid 40's and attractive, are
carrying stacks of legal files to their Escort Wagon.

                    AARON
          Hey, Mr. And Mrs. S.!

                    MR. SHIPMAN
               (faux enthusiasm)
          Oh look, it's Aaron.

                    MRS. SHIPMAN
               (covering, but just
                barely)
          Hello Aaron.

                    AARON
          Can I help?

                    MRS. SHIPMAN
          No, we're fine, really. Stay in
          your vehicle.

Torrance bounds out of the front door, carrying practice
gear. She kisses her dad en route to Aaron's truck.

                    TORRANCE
          Bye! Be back later!

                    MR. & MRS. SHIPMAN
          Bye.

The Shipmans watch her run off, share a look, then continue
to load up the car.

6/9/99   7.

                         AARON
                      (continuing)
            Trust me. You're gonna get it.

He gives her a big sexy smile. Torrance musters a smile of
her own, then nods understandingly. She grabs her gear and
hops out.

                         TORRANCE
            Bye.

Aaron blows her a kiss, then blazes off in the Tracker. As
Torrance watches him go, Kasey passes by her.

                         KASEY
            You're so lucky, Torrance.

                         TORRANCE
                      (not so sure)
            Yeah...

LESLIE, one of the male cheerleaders, joins Torrance as the
others disperse. They walk toward practice together.

                         LESLIE
            Just cause all those idiots
            worship him doesn't mean you have
            to stay with him, y'know?

                         TORRANCE
            I believe the word you're looking
            for is loyalty?

                         LESLIE
            Then you put the oy in loyalty

> Calm down with the word play, JB. Nice try with OY but it's not happening.

                         TORRANCE
            Nice splice.

17   INT. LOCKER ROOM - DAY   17

A LOCKER DOOR slams. Girls are in various states of undress.
Our main girls (Whitney, Courtney, Darcy, Carver and Kasey)
are getting dressed for practice. Tape winds around
stomachs, beneath bras. Ankle braces go on under socks;
flesh-colored knee braces; wrist tape and guards; lower back
belts; double sports bras. Speculation fills the air.

                         WHITNEY
            Did you vote?

                         COURTNEY
            Yeah. Darcy thinks she should get
            Captain because her dad pays for
            everything.

6/9/99   8.

                    WHITNEY
          She also thinks she can pull off
          orange lipstick.

IN ANOTHER PART OF THE LOCKER ROOM

                    KASEY
          Courtney'll get captain. The guys
          love clutching her butt.

                    DARCY
          There is a lot to hang onto.
          What's the plural for butt? On
          one person, I mean.

                    CARVER
          She puts the ass in massive.

Darcy checks out Carver's sizeable rear end.

                    DARCY
          And you put the lude in deluded.

Big Red appears, holding a list. Everyone immediately snaps
to attention.

                    BIG RED
          Yo! Do I have all your votes?

COACH SHELTON, their 42-year-old bubble-headed advisor, pops
her head in.

                    COACH SHELTON
          Gimme those votes! C'mon, squad!

The girls hand their slips to Big Red who ambles off with
Coach Shelton. The squad rolls their eyes collectively.

                    DARCY
          Five whole seconds of coaching!
          We have a new world record!
             (to Kasey)
          I guess you don't have to have a
          head to be a figure-head.

Torrance appears.

                    TORRANCE
          We should've gotten Big Red a
          gift. Someone should say something.

Courtney and Whitney exchange loaded glances.

                    COURTNEY
          Pass.

Body shaming as sport. Sad but true and glad this is changing.

Hello and goodbye, Coach Shelton. Your services are no longer needed but we wish you well, whoever you are.

6/9/99   9.

WHITNEY
Good riddance. I don't believe in
assmosis.

TORRANCE
I am not brown-nosing! She's the
departing captain. Come on. You
both sucked before she whipped you
into shape.

COURTNEY
Whipped? Oh, that's what that was.

WHITNEY
No one will miss Big Red, Tor.
She puts the itch in bitch.

COURTNEY
She puts the whore in horrifying.

TORRANCE
It's her last practice with us!
How would you feel?

COURTNEY
Big Red has no feelings.

WHITNEY
Just testicles.

KASEY
          (to no one in
          particular)
Hey, is it true they're coming out
with Diet Evian?

DARCY
Yeah. It has fewer calories than
air.

KASEY
Air has calories?

DARCY
Yeah, but not as many as non-Diet
Evian.

KASEY
I am never drinking regular water
again.

Big Red appears again, clapping her hands furiously.

BIG RED
Let's do this, children! Outside!
Now!

175

6/13/97   p.18

                    WHITNEY
          She's not gonna do it.

                    TORRANCE
          It's so mean. (sarcastic) But hey: if you
          can't flush your values down the toilet,
          what can you flush down the toilet?

                    JAN
          You can mop <u>handle</u> it.

                    WHITNEY
                 (irritated)
          Broom handle!

> Everyone relax. Just some spirit stick humor, it's going to be ok. Maybe not but no one freak out.

Torrance grabs a CAMERA and heads over to the winner's table.

NEW POPE TABLE - CONTINUOUS

The New Pope SQUAD is excited to see her and greet her with
southern syrup.

                    NEW POPE GIRL #1
          Y'all were brighter than silver dollars
          today, my goodness! Y'all are such an
          inspiration to us, I mean it!

                    TORRANCE
          I just wanted to congratulate you guys, and
          get a picture of you...with the Spirit
          Stick.

The squad hits an ornate formation in seconds flat, Torrance
grabs the SS, handing it over.

                    TORRANCE
          Here, you hold it --

Accidentally/on-purpose, Torrance passes the stick too
quickly, letting it fall --

IN SLO MO: Four New Pope girls fly through the air - as if
the stick is a grenade - to prevent it from touching the
ground.

NEW POPE FACES faces distort in genuine horror, silent
screams of agony, as the Spirit Stick hits the floor with an
echoing CRACK, RIBBONS AND SEQUINS flying everywhere.

> As written, y'all.

IN REAL TIME: The messhall is quiet. As the collective GASPS
OF HORROR, outrage and shock reverb through the room.

Torrance picks up the stick and attempts to hand it to a New
Pope cheerleader.

>   NEW POPE CHEERLEADER #1
>   I don't want it now.

>   NEW POPE CHEERLEADER #2
>   It's okay. It's fine. The Spirit Stick
>   doesn't lose anything, the person who drops
>   it, however...goes to Hades. We all are
>   fine. (to her squad) We are fine.

TORRANCE is white with guilt and remorse. Normal DIN
resumes, as if nothing happened.

A FLASH goes off behind Torrance's head. NP SQUAD disperses,
SNICKERING at some inside joke. An NP Cheerio seethes,
handing Torrance her camera.

>   NEW POPE CHEERLEADER #3
>   I am a Phillips-head, and you are screwed,
>   sister.

10   EXT. MINI VAN - CALIFORNIA - DAY - ESTABLISHING   10

The VAN blows down a four-lane, passing a CITY LIMITS SIGN
that reads: *WELCOME TO SANTA ANA, CALIFORNIA -- HOME OF THE
FILIAS DEUS TITANS, FIVE-TIME NATIONAL CHEERLEADING
CHAMPIONS.*

11   INT. MINI VAN - CONTINUOUS   11

Torrance is squeezed into the van with Darcy, Jan and other
SQUAD MEMBERS, staring as the sign whizzes by. Darcy's mom,
MRS. ESTRADA, 48, drives and chuckles rudely.

>   MRS. ESTRADA
>   So, captain, huh? Not too much pressure,
>   huh, Torrance? It's never too late if you
>   don't feel up to it, you know?

>   TORRANCE
>   I was born to feel up to it.

>   MRS. ESTRADA
>   There's no shame in knowing your
>   limitations.

>   DARCY
>   Shut up, mom.

Torrance flips through her funsaver PHOTOS, shocked by what
she sees:

6/9/99   32.

> TORRANCE
> I don't have any video!

> MISSY
> We're clean.

Isis sizes them up. It's a tense moment. Then...

> LAVA
> Come on, Isis, you the mack diva.
> You let 'em know.

Torrance and Missy back away and head for the car.

This is corny - I was experimenting with the campiness and it's not coming across as campy. Just forced.

> LAVA
> (continuing)
> They leavin'.

> JENELOPE
> (testifying)
> Let the car door hit you where the
> good lord split you!

> CLOVERS
> Buh-bye/Seeya!/Go on back to Diego!

As Missy's car pulls away, Isis turns to the Clovers.

"God as my witness" is my fave line in a Foo Fighters song but - again - was going for camp and it's falling flat.

> ISIS
> (intense)
> I've been standing by watching
> this shit for too long. Now that
> I'm Captain, it's all gonna
> change. As god as my witness, we
> are going to Nationals this year.

54   INT. MISSY'S CAR - NIGHT   54

Torrance is really shattered. Missy registers this.

> MISSY
> You really had no idea, did you?

> TORRANCE
> (shaking her head)
> Do you know what ths means? My
> entire cheerleading career has
> been a lie. Every routine, every
> trophy -- a lie.

> MISSY
> (lightly)
> Look on the bright side: it's only
> cheerleading.

6/9/99   33.

                    TORRANCE
          I am 'only cheerleading'.

So much better here and one of my fave lines.

Missy looks at her and sees that she means it.

                    TORRANCE
                 (continuing)
          Can I ask you something?

                    MISSY
          Hit me.

                    TORRANCE
          Do you believe in curses?

                    MISSY
          Only with regard to menstruation.

I still enjoy this Missy line. Eliza would've crushed this.

                    TORRANCE
          No, seriously. I think I'm cursed.

                    MISSY
          And why's that?

                    TORRANCE
          This summer? At cheer camp? All
          the new seniors had to do a haze --

SCARY MUSIC swells as we...

                                        FLASHBACK TO:

55   INT. CAMP LOCATION CAFETERIA - NIGHT   55

     Ecu: the spirit stick

ECU should be all caps, Jess. Jeez.

                    BIG RED
                 (whisper to Torrance)
          As is FDS tradition, each senior
          must submit to an induction ritual
          as specified by me. Torrance
          Shipman: Your mission should you
          choose to accept it -- and you'd
          better -- is to capture the Spirit
          Stick...

In tact - it's so crazy to see this... Was around from jump, although at one point the movie opened at camp. This scene is much better as a flashback after Missy is introduced.

Bid Red eyes the other squad members with an evil grin.

                    BIG RED
                 (continuing)
          ...and drop it! In front of the
          entire camp.

Torrance is appalled, looking like she just watched someone
eat their own barf.

6/9/99   34.

> TORRANCE
> The Spirit Stick can't touch the
> ground! Or it will lose all its
> spirit! And even if it is a
> totally bogus concept, it's bad
> sportsmanship.

This scene is also better here. Thank you, Peyton.

> BIG RED
> Torrance, the Spirit Stick is not
> your friend. In fact, it's what
> makes people hate cheerleaders.
> It's girlish and frivolous, and you
> must rob it of its power.
> 'Sportsmen' don't need stupid
> sticks when they've got discipline
> and dedication. You're an athlete
> first, and a cheerleader second. I
> hope you're not forgetting that.
> Choose: the squad or the stick.

Big Red is really aggressive about public perception, which is not surprising given what she's been getting away with? Appearances mean a lot to her... safe to say?

> NEW POPE SQUAD (B.G.)
> J-E-S-U-S, He's the one we love
> the best, Jesus, yeah, yeah, Jesus!

Torrance grudgingly heads over to the winner's table.

56   INT. NEW POPE TABLE - CONTINUOUS   56

The New Pope SQUAD is excited to see her and greet her with
southern syrup.

> NEW POPE GIRL #1
> Y'all are such an inspiration to
> us, I mean it!

> TORRANCE
> I just wanted to congratulate you
> guys. And get a picture of you...
> with the Spirit Stick.

The squad hits an ornate formation in seconds flat. Torrance
grabs the Stick, handing it over.

> TORRANCE
> (continuing)
> Here, you hold it --

Accidentally/on-purpose, Torrance passes the Stick too
quickly, letting it fall --

IN SLO MO: Four New Pope girls fly through the air - as if
the stick is a grenade - to prevent it from touching the
ground.

6/9/99   35.

NEW POPE FACES distort in genuine horror, silent screams of
agony, as the Spirit Stick hits the floor with an echoing
CRACK, RIBBONS AND SEQUINS flying everywhere.

IN REAL TIME: The mess hall is quiet as the collective GASPS
OF HORROR, OUTAGE and SHOCK reverb through the room.

Torrance picks up the Stick and attempts to hand it to a
nervous New Pope cheerleader.

> I love the delivery on these lines.

                    NEW POPE CHEERLEADER #1
          I don't want it now.

                    NEW POPE CHEERLEADER #2
          It's okay. It's fine. The Spirit
          Stick doesn't lose anything. The
          person who drops it, however...
               (with spite)
          ...goes to Hades.

> Trivia time: Line delivered by Cybil Shepherd's daughter - like the rest of America, I loved MOONLIGHTING.

                                        FLASHFORWARD TO:

57   INT. MISSY'S CAR - NIGHT   57

Missy looks at Torrance, laughing.

                    MISSY
          I don't mean to laugh, but
          'cheerleading urban legend'?

Torrance throws her a look that means business. Missy shakes
her head.

                    MISSY
               (continuing)
          You're not jinxed. Shit happens.

> Line works better here, and Eliza Dushku really sells it.

58   EXT. FREEWAY - NIGHT   58

Missy's car blazes back to San Diego.

59   INT. SHIPMAN LIVING ROOM - NIGHT   59

Torrance enters, ashen-faced and makes a beeline for the
phone. As she dials, Justin enters and promptl farts.

                    TORRANCE
               (annoyed)
          C'mon creep!

> Why do something PROMPTLY when you can PROMPTL?

181

6/13/97   p.23

NATIONALS, spaces in between filled with *PRACTICE, WEIGHT TRAINING, TUMBLING*; or *HOME/AWAY GAME*).

This is overkill, and not the good kind. Too many subplots.

As her printer HUMS, we zoom in on the entry form Tor's filling out: *American Cheerleader's* **CHEERLEADER OF THE MONTH** contest.

EXT. FDS SOCCER FIELD - DAY   16

Kasey (whose hair is now blue) and Darcy approach the field in tandem.

                    KASEY
          Will you teach me the SAT cheer?

                    DARCY
          Math or verbal?

                    KASEY
          Verbal, I guess.

                    DARCY
          Okay, it goes word then definition, word
          then definition in one long, run-on sentence
          cheer. It's more cheer-singing than
          cheerleading.

Jan approaches, joining the group.

                    KASEY
          Hit me.

                    DARCY
          Part one, here we go:
                    (clapping in 4/4 time, raising
                    her hands like Evita on each
                    SAT word for emphasis)
          Turgid - I'm bloated but/ I'm Tensile,
          withstanding stress and /Tantamount's
          equivalent while /Paramount is dominant/
          Quotidian is daily, don't get /Querulous -
          complaining, try Qui/escence - that's
          stillness be a /Sybarite - a pleasure
          seeker, /Recondite - few know it, I'm
          Vo/ciferous - loud, vocal but not/ Wizened -
          that's wrinkled/we'll end on tenesmus.

I am proud of this cheer but I doubt any of these are SAT words anymore?

See: DVD extras.

                    KASEY
          What's tenesmus?

                    DARCY
          The unsuccessful straining associated with
          the urgent need to number one or number two.

> DARCY
> It's a person or thing with great size and
> power. As for what they do, you'd know
> better than I would.

WARM-UP MONTAGE: Extreme partner stretching, pushing and
nudging each other into amazing pretzel-like shapes. Guys on
backs, doing presses with girls standing in their cupped
hands, hitting various stunt positions. These guys are Chas
Atlas strong, making goofy noises - BURPS, GRUNTS, FARTS -
and pretending the girls are too heavy.

Charles Atlas was a famous bodybuilder.

> TORRANCE
> Okay, let's do this. This is untested, but
> I'd like to try a Wolf's Wall.

The squad erupts into LAUGHTER. Courtney puts a palm on T's
forehead, checking for fever.

> KASEY
> What's a Wolf's Wall?

> LESLEY
> The hardest pyramid known to cheerleader.

> DARCY
> The words 'big' and 'britches' come to mind.

> TORRANCE
> Come on! Where's your drive?

> JAN
> In my car.

> DARCY
> Let us graduate in one piece, shall we?

> COURTNEY
> You guys suck. Let's do this.

> WHITNEY
> Trust! Let us rock the stunt, por favor!

The squad GRUMBLES agreement.

> CARVER
> Can I fly?

> DARCY
> Turgid.

> JAN
> She's too heavy.

                    TORRANCE
          Yeah, but she's not scared.

They try the "build" once. It crumbles. They go a second
time, it wobbles and falls. A third time, they almost nail
it. Fourth time, they stick it.

CARVER'S POV: from the top of the pyramid. Looking down,
three body lengths high, we feel the vertigo. It's high.

DOWN BELOW: the guys are straining. Veins popping from all
the bodies they're holding. THEIR POV: Legs, butts, crotches.

                    LESLEY
          Pinch some pennies, someone's slacking.

This is a legit cheerleading term from the 90s.

                    JAN
          This weight is gonna push my arm straight up
Foreshadowing? through someone's poop-shoot in one hot
          second --

                    TORRANCE
          Carver, can you full out?

                    CARVER
          Yup!

From Carver's POV again, the camera spins through the air,
falling, falling, falling... then a thud. BLOOD-CURDLING
SCREAM.

17   EXT. AMBULANCE   17

EMERGENCY MEDICAL TECHNICIANS load Carver - on a stretcher -
into the vehicle. In the background,

FOUR PERMED-OUT GIRLS *Too much. Too many subplots. Too many things.*

with gargantuan pom pons strut, primp and pose, LAUGHING in
disbelief. It's the Filias Deus Dazzlers, a drill-team and
pompon combo. The Dazzlers are walking leaflets re: the evils
of make-up.

                    JAN
          Eww. The Tonya Hardings are here.

                    PAM ANNE
          How's the yodeling, Heidis?

                    JAN
          Now, now. Don't use words you can't spell.
          But for the record, 'the' is T-H-E. That   *This joke was moved to misspelled LEG.*
          should come in handy.

                    PAM ANNE
         Jan, anytime your ready for a real woman,
         you know who to call.

                    LESLEY
         Pam Anne, real women don't consider sequins
         a daily fashion food-group.

                    JAN
         Ohmigod! Pam Anne, are you sick? Your neck
         is a different color than your jawline!
         (miming phone) Hello? Get me Estee Lauder,
         stat! We have a code blue!

    Pam Anne looks at her squadmates with concern, her face - in
    fact - is five shades darker than her neck.

                    PAM ANNE
         Like I need make-up.

18   INT. KITCHEN - NIGHT   18

    Torrance is on top of Justin, pinning him and holding a fork
    to Justin's nostril.

                    JUSTIN
               (bored)
         Please, master of the universe, pick my nose
         and feed me my buggers. (beat) Simply
         because you consider snot an appetizer,
         doesn't mean it runs in the family --

                    MRS. SHIPMAN (O.S.)
         Torrance, get off your brother.

                    TORRANCE
         I got captain.

    Mom picks up an envelope and official-looking paper.

                    MRS. SHIPMAN
               (not listening)
         What? Oh. This blistering academic
         schedule shouldn't get in your way. You must
         be very happy.

                    TORRANCE
         Why can't you accept the fact that I am not
         a genius? It just kills you that I'm not an
         honor student.

> *This is just weird since Les is out. I guess I was trying to make her very clueless and Jan very mean?*

> *"Blistering" makes me smile.*

> *As written. :-)*

185

6/13/97   p.28

                    MRS. SHIPMAN
          You could be. Average effort yields average
          gains. Your priorities are -- never mind.
          (changing tactics) College might less of a
          shock if you take an extra lab or language
          course. What do you think?

                    TORRANCE
          Will advanced chem get you off my back?

                    MRS. SHIPMAN
          Not completely, but it'll help.

                    TORRANCE
          Done. You know, mothers have killed to get
          their daughters on squads.

                    MRS. SHIPMAN
          That mother didn't kill anyone, she hired a
          hit man. It is only cheerleading, and I
          think I keep it in perspective. Try it
          sometime.

                    TORRANCE
          It is my very last, first day of high school
          tomorrow, thank you for all the maternal
          dotage.

     Feelings hurt, Torrance storms off to her room. A door SLAMS.
     Mrs. Shipman sighs and returns to her depositions.

19   EXT./INT. VARIOUS - DAY   19

     FIRST DAY OF SCHOOL MONTAGE:

     YELLOW BUSES spewing forth STUDENTS. CARS, MOPEDS and
     SKATEBOARDS pulling up to

20   EXT. FILIAS DEUS SCHOOL FRONT STEPS   20

     Kids hanging out in CLIQUES. LES sits alone, in cheer gear.
     TWO FOOTBALL PLAYERS walk by.

                    FDS TIGHT END
          Whoo! Sexy, Lesley.

                    FDS QUARTERBACK
          Hey, fag.

     Torrance appears.

> Wild that this was always there - I think the inverted dynamic (not caring about cheerleading) really works and the parents nonchalance was beautifully played.

> This is a reference to THE POSITIVELY TRUE ADVENTURES OF THE ALLEGED TEXAS CHEERLEADER MURDERING MOM, directed by one of the all-time greats, Michael Ritchie.

6/13/97   p.35

>   DARCY
>   Bring on the tyros, the neophytes and
>   dilettanti!
>
>   JAN
>   SAT's are over, Darcy.
>
>   DARCY
>   I can go for 800 verbal if I so desire.

26   EXT./INT. GYMNASIUM - CONTINUOUS   26

TRYOUT MONTAGE:

Quick cuts of the array of AUDITIONERS: Shaking smiles; too
stiff; too quiet; too scared; too over the top; too bizarre.

JAMIE, a ridiculously tiny freshman, breezes through her
try-out unspectacularly, WINKING at the squad when she
finishes.

Last but not least, a STRAGGLER walks in. A brunette 16
year-old wearing low-slung chollo trousers, a sleeveless
white undershirt with dayglow bra straps hanging out, and
some ornately hi-tech Nikes. A baroque black tattoo rings
around one bicep. MISSY PANTONE looks more like a roadie for
Social Distortion than a cheerleading candidate, but looks
are deceiving.

(How much do we love Missy?)

>   COURTNEY
>   Tattoos are strictly verboten. Sorry.

(I MEAN...!) Missy licks her middle finger thoroughly, and just when you
think she's going to flash it, she runs it over the tattoo,
smearing it.

>   MISSY
>   I got bored during fourth period. Can I
>   still try out?
>
>   WHITNEY
>   You need to fill this out --
>
>   MISSY
>   (producing form)
>   Did it.

Missy drops her long-chain-key-chain to the floor with a
CLUNK.

187

                    TORRANCE
                (looks at form)
        Missy? Before we start, I'm afraid we need to
        make sure you can do a standing back tuck.

                    MISSY
        Standing full okay?

Missy quickly executes a standing, full-twisting back layout.
It's Miller time. Shannon Miller.

> Shannon Miller is an Olympic gymnast.

> Okay, gymnastic nerds; I know this combination makes zero sense. A brandy is a no-handed round-off and impossible to generate momentum, I believe. I liked the way "Brandy" sounded.

                    WHITNEY
                (challenge)
        Brandy, back-handspring, whipback, whipback,
        tuck out.

Missy flies into the tumbling pass before Whitney's done
reciting it. Hammers it.

                    COURTNEY
        But can she yell? Where's she from?

                    MISSY
                (screaming, cheer-like)
        What? I transferred from Los Angeles.

> This got much better next pass.

Various squad members wince from the volume.

                    TORRANCE
        Jan'll show you a cheer - and you do it
        back?

                    JAN
        Awesome-ohwow --

                    MISSY
                (joining)
        liketotallyfreakmeoutImeanforsure, righton,
        the Titans sure are number one!

> Thank you, Kayla Alpert.

Folks are impressed.

                    JAN
        Okay: Crunch, crunch!--

                    MISSY
                (joining)
        We'll eat you up for lunch! Score, score!
        We'll wipe you on the floor!
        How bout a death press?

6/13/97   p.37

                    WHITNEY
Death presses were outlawed by ACA seven
years ago.

                    JAN
                 (jumps up)
I'll do it with you!

Missy stands facing Jan - the duo semi-plie. Missy places
both hands on Jan's head, he squats, flips her upside down as
she presses up into a handstand. On his head. The squad's
groan of contentment stops -- when Missy removes one hand.
Sports fans: Missy Pantone is doing a one-armed handstand on
Jan's noggin.

(Is it worth mentioning this is excessive?)

(Also: STICK IT.)

                    TORRANCE
                 (to squad)
Missy is bank.

                    COURTNEY
No she's not. We have all already soooo
decided on Jamie!

                    WHITNEY
Screw Jamie.

                    LESLEY
And the horse she rode in on.

                    TORRANCE
Guys?

                    GUYS
We love her/No brainer/Duh - she rules/Jamie
sucked.

                    TORRANCE
Courtney, this is not a democracy. It's a
cheer-ocracy. I'm sorry, but we're
over-ruling you!

(Ta da!!)

                    COURTNEY
The word is Cheer-tatorship. You're being a
cheer-tator, Torrance. We already voted!
Besides, Missy looks like an uber-dyke.

(Courtney is using a slur. She's not the nicest character, as you may have surmised.)

This is not lost on Missy.

                    DARCY
Excellent use of uber. However, I optate
her.

(As written.)

A door SLAMS. Missy's gone.

189

>   TORRANCE
> Courtney, I'm captain. I'm pulling rank, and
> you can fall in line or not. If we're gonna
> be the best, we have to have the best, and
> she's the best! Missy's the poo, so take a
> big whiff.

Let me just say: bravo, Bendinger. Self love.

27   EXT. PANTONE HOUSE - NIGHT   27

Torrance rings a DOORBELL. The door opens, changing
Torrance's demeanor noticeably. Hard to tell why until we
see

CLIFF from the cafeteria. Foreigner t-shirt, baggy chinos and
buzzed hair, his eyes smile. Torrance is frozen. They snatch
mutual stares.

>   CLIFF
> Welcome wagon?

>   TORRANCE
> Hi. Does Missy live here?

>   CLIFF
> She moved back to LA. Something about witchy
> teenage cheerleaders --

>   TORRANCE
> No - she's perfect. We loved her! We have
> to get her!

>   CLIFF
> Is her drug dependency going to be a
> problem?

So happy that joke stayed.

Missy appears at the door.

>   MISSY
> Cliff - shut up.

>   TORRANCE
> We want you! You're the best and they know
> it. Courtney's just threatened because you
> rock so damn hard, she'll come around.

>   MISSY
> No way. No thanks.

>   TORRANCE
> Please? Can I say or do or promise anything
> to get you to reconsider? Seriously!
> (manic) Say yes, say yes, say yes!

6/13/97   p.41

                    MISSY
              (super-bitch)
    I know all the routines already.

                  TORRANCE
    No-rexia!

                    MISSY
    Torrance, I know them because I've seen them
    for years. Everything's ripped off. I want
    no slice of this pie.

                  TORRANCE
    This is your brain on drugs. I fought to
    get you on the squad, if you've changed your
    mind at least be cool about it, don't make
    shit up.

                    MISSY
    This bambina wants none of the thievery,
    chica.

> I thought maybe Missy imported some LA lingo but it's too much like Toros' speak and doesn't really work.

                  TORRANCE
    I don't understand.

MONTAGE TO ROCKIN' MUZAK:

> There is no such thing as "Rockin' Muzak." I don't even know what this joke is about.

30   EXT. 5 FREEWAY; EXT. 91 FREEWAY; EXT. 405 FREEWAY   30

                  TORRANCE
              (lost)
        You and hoo, where are we going? Could I get
        a destination? An ETA? A raison to etre?

> This is a bit of a shout-out to CLUELESS.

A CITY LIMITS SIGN

reads: *Welcome to the City of INGLEWOOD*. From the looks of
things, we have left the Emerald City for the wrong side of
the tracks

31   INT. CLIFF'S CADILLAC   31

Torrance stares at the sign, concerned.

> I don't think the mascot has gotten enough love. I love the leprechaun. #proud
>
> What no one has discussed is the how Irish cultural tuff is foisted upon the Clovers and they deal vs. Toros, who steal.

                  TORRANCE
        Anglebranch? Angletree? Inglewood?

32   INT. INGLEWOOD HS GYMNASIUM

THE MASCOT

is an orange leprechaun picking a green four-leaf clover.
Ancient, the fourth leaf has cracked and is hanging on by a

6/13/97   p.42

thread. Welcome to Inglewood High School, home of the
Inglewood Clovers.

Second quarter of a GIRLS B-BALL GAME finishes up. BUZZER
sounds. Torrance, Cliff and Missy stand beside a bleacher.
The SPECTATORS start STOMPING and WHISTLING.

> Cliff was there? Weird.

SEVEN GIRLS and SEVEN GUYS - the predominantly
African-American Inglewood Clovers Cheerleading squad -
stroll onto the court wearing baggy layers of hip hop gear.
They're disorganized and pretty lackadaisical. LAUGHING,
elbowing each other, having fun.

The CAPTAIN, whose shirt reads 'O MIGHTY ISIS' flings her
braids and raises her arms like a conductor. The group falls
silent.

                    ISIS
          I said Brrrr, it's cold in here -

> I first saw this at a step competition in New York City at Columbia University in the late 80s. "Brrr" is a famous step cadence.

TORRANCE looks shocked.

> Uncle Google indicates Alpha Phi Alpha are the originators of "Brrr."

The entire CLOVER SQUAD begins an Byzantine stepping
sequence, featuring INTRICATE STOMPING & CLAPPING RHYTHMS.
The squad strips down their clothing - revealing hip green
and orange uniforms underneath. Gals in lycra hot pants,
kneepads, crop tops with chenille 'I's on the bust. Guys in
pegleg Adidas pants and baggy jerseys.

TORRANCE covers her mouth in sheer panic.

Fast NRG HOUSE MUSIC begins. The squad LAUGHS and relaxes for
a bar, then launches into a one-minute dance sequence. Part
Lindy, part vaudeville/circus act and jitterbug, the Clovers
explode with pure creative energy. They are fiercely
original, even though it's the same routine Tor and Company
just did. Only better. Much, much, better.

MISSY looks at TORRANCE with concern. Tor shakes her head,
bites a nail and clutches her stomach at the same time.

Girls doing headstands on boys heads; Boys doing backflip
tosses out of girls cupped palms; High-fiving each other in
the air mid-toss. It is one minute of pure, unadulterated,
fun. The CROWD goes wild with APPLAUSE.

                    TORRANCE
          I'm in hell. Get me home.

In his *Foghat* shirt, Cliff leads the trio --

> Apparently, I cannot resist the opportunity to throw in an unnecessary rock and roll T-shirt. Please ignore this tendency.

6/13/97   p.43

33   EXT. INGLEWOOD HIGH SCHOOL PARKING LOT   33

out to the car. They're almost there, when Isis clamps a paw
onto Tor's FDS Letter Jacket. Isis has TWO CLOVER COHORTS,
LAVA and JENELOPE.

                    ISIS
        Ex-squeeze me, but I have to call you out.

                    LAVA
        We are ready to boot up, y'all.

                    TORRANCE
        Uh wow. Hi. You guys were great.

                    ISIS
                (dripping)
        No? Really? You ready to share the trophy?
        Where's Bozo? The clown with her very own
        camera --

                    MISSY
        Bozo?

                    ISIS
                (to Missy)
        This is an A and B conversation, and you can
        C your way out of it, thank you.
                (to Torrance)
        Big, ugly Red-head. Video camera. Been
        snakin our routines for years. We just love
        seeing them on ESPN.

                    TORRANCE
        I'm not sure, uh, you know, about that --

                    ISIS
        Oohsaywadewa - Brrr, it's cold in here I
        said there must be some Titans in the
        atmosphere. You think a white girl thought
        that shit up?

                    TORRANCE
        I didn't think anything, quite honestly.

                    ISIS
        Ouch!   There's a new knife in town and she
        is sha-arp!

Isis is livid, and in Tor's face.

"Oohsaywadewa" is an urban cheer/cadence I cannot find anywhere. If anyone knows or remembers this cadence or can find it, LMK.

Irony not lost on me in 1997. Or now.

Pat shoves Darcy off his shoulder.

                    PAT
                (accusatory)
        Why is my shoulder damp?   (Bye, Pat. Your joke is gross.)

JAN holds onto MISSY by the waist, preparing to do a lift.
They prep and dip: Jan lifts, and as they hit the move...we
see Jan holding only THE SKIRT over his head.

MISSY, still ground-bound, wears only spankies and her
uniform top. She grabs the skirt from Jan.

COURTNEY AND BROOKE do the same lift. As Courtney nails her
'chair', her eyes pop out.

Brooke grins wolfishly, his hand clearly holding her by the
butt.   Courtney WHOOPS and jumps out of her stunt early.

Brooke smells his thumb and smiles. An ANTI-BAC WIPE appears
out of thin air.

IN THE BLEACHERS

ISIS & THREE Inglewood CLOVERS enter the football field,
sneaking into top row of the bleachers undetected.

Immediately, Inglewood begins copying FDS' sideline cheers.
They imitate moves from the stands, eliciting a small bit of
attention. The quartet move down a few rows.

ON THE SIDELINES

Torrance is immediately ruffled. Missy grabs Tor.

                    MISSY
        Just ignore them.

FRONT ROW BLEACHERS

Isis and company squeeze down into front row and imitate FDS
in a bigger way, CACKLING. Inglewood's fierce foursome stand
in front of FDS.

CLIFF'S capturing everything on Kodak paper.   (Remember cameras?)

SIDELINE IN PROFILE

INGLEWOOD and FDS are face to face, in show-down mode. A
group human mirror, both squads perform the cheers. The
Clovers mimic the FDS chant perfectly. The entire FDS squad
gets tighter and louder in response. The Clovers rise to the
challenge of being outnumbered: they are fierce.

6/13/97   p.60

                    COURTNEY
                 (re. Clovers)
     Nagging itch and embarassing odor!

> This is a reference to a very embarrassing FDS (feminine deodorant spray) commercial. I have no words.

                    WHITNEY
     Is anyone else freaking out? How do they
     know all our shit?

                    TORRANCE
     I'll tell you later. Quick: Let's do "ooh."

Isis' group dominate the cheer in a deliverance-style case of
one-upmanship. The Clovers turn and face the audience.

                    CLOVERS
     Ooh ooh zip zoom zow, flash more points on
     the scoreboard now. Ooh ooh zip zoom zow --

                    TORRANCE
                 (yelling over)
     Pick-up backs on three! One, two --

Inglewood falls silent. Like a marine drill team: one third
of the FDS kids start the drill by nailing standing back
tucks (SBT); Immediately, two thirds of the squad launched
into a second SBT; For the finale, the entire FDS squad
nails a simultaneous back flip.

FDS squad stands at attention, staring defiantly at the
Clovers. Isis retaliates, raising her conductor arms.

                    ISIS
     Achoo! Bless you!

                    CLOVERS
     Do our bit/ you'll look like shit/ cuz we
     the ones who/ down with it/ You better hide/
     you should have fear/cuz we will kick your
     ass this year!

> From pitch to final cut. #proud

                    ISIS
                 (normal)
     You know, we never even tried to go for
     those bull-shit nationals before. But this
     year, as God is my secret judge, we will be
     there. We are coming just to wax your ass,
     Titans! So watch your back.

The Clovers storm off with a flourish. CLIFF snaps away.

                    DARCY
     Torrance? Explanation. Prontissimo!

195

6/9/99   51.

Both Torrance and Cliff react to this, thinking that's talking to them. Torrance exits, a little flustered.

>   TORRANCE
>   Oh, I was just...I have to brush
>   my teeth.

Missy looks at Cliff, annoyed.

>   MISSY
>   Don't do what you always do --

>   CLIFF
>   I don't always do anything.

>   MISSY
>   Just my best friend.

>   CLIFF
>   This theme is tired, Miss.

>   MISSY
>   I didn't choose you, you I have to
>   live with. But I choose my friends.

>   CLIFF
>   And we both have great taste.

>   MISSY
>   If it's all about you have sex with
>   Torrance tell me now so I can quit.

>   CLIFF
>   You know what? I thought it would
>   be good for you to, like, meet
>   people and not be some tragic
>   outsider. But I was wrong. You
>   make friends so easily. I was
>   stupid to worry. You should quit.

>   MISSY
>   Do you have any idea what it feels
>   like to be on the receiving end of
>   your jilting? You date my
>   friends, get sick of them, break
>   their hearts and who gets the
>   blame? That's right! Me! And
>   Cliff has no remorse whatsoever.
>   I am not your pimp. So stop
>   treating my social life like it's
>   your personal dating service. Back
>   off. I'm serious.

>   CLIFF
>   When have I ever listened to you?

The Cliff lothario and Cliff/Missy sibling tension lives for this draft only. Enjoy.

This is over-written. It's always a bad sign when you are putting expository history inside the dialogue itself. There was a very "self-aware" referential thing in the Buffy era, but it's not tracking anymore and needed to get refined.

6/9/99   52.

Frustrated, Missy stalks back to her bedroom, throwing a look into the bathroom as she passes it.

84   INT. PANTONE BATHROOM - CONTINUOUS   84

Torrance, brushing her teeth, looks back at Missy and smiles awkwardly.

85   INT. CLIFF'S ROOM - CONTINUOUS   85

Cliff heads out of his room.

86   INT. PANTONE BATHROOM - CONTINUOUS   86

Cliff joins Torrance at the sink, totally ignoring her. Torrance is taken by surprise.

Cliff unscrews the toothpaste cape, squeezing the toothpaste onto the bristles. He turns on the water. She rinses, shutting it off. He turns the faucet back on. She rinses, shutting it off. She spits. He spits. A playful interlude, bursting with romantic tension. He rinses and spits again, wiping his mouth and giving her a huge smile before exiting.

> Hello, toothbrush scene. Written in my apartment in West Hollywood with Peyton at my side, egging me on.

> Peyton felt the fast pacing needed a moment to breathe and ventilate. We discussed IT HAPPENED ONE NIGHT, and I'd been watching HIS GIRL FRIDAY.

87   INT. MISSY'S BEDROOM - CONTINUOUS   87

Missy is awake, propped up, as Torrance enters.

                    MISSY
          Are you into my brother?

                    TORRANCE
               (yes)
          No! I have a boyfriend.

With that, she switches the light out. And we see Missy and Torrance both staring at the ceiling, thinking...

88   INT. MISSY'S BEDROOM - NEXT MORNING   88

Torrance sits on Missy's bed with Missy beside her. She picks up the phone and dials.

                    TORRANCE
               (continuing)
          Hello? Aaron?

6/13/97   p.74

This time, boys toss her and Courtney lays out and opens her
legs and arms into an X.

GUYS POV: is all crotch.

                    SPARKY
          Oh my.

When the guys go to catch her, Les misses one of her legs.

                    SPARKY
               (to Les)
          Take off your skirt, Sally. Catch her like
          a man or go home.

                    LESLEY
               (to Jan)
          Nothing like a homophobic homosexual.

> This was meant to contrast the pain of younger/older gay generation gap by using the closet/self-loathing to make a point, but it doesn't work. Cut!

Sparky hears this and crosses his arms.

                    SPARKY
               (to Les)
          I hate to break it to you, Nancy, but I'm
          engaged. To a woman.

                    COACH SHELTON
               (oblivious)
          You are? She's a lucky gal.

                    MISSY
               (to Tor)
          Or dresses just like one.

SPARKY demonstrates a move, making corny jazz hands.

                    WHITNEY
          Can we lose the sparkle fingers?

                    SPARKY
          Spirit fingers. Spirit fingers, young lady,
          are a classic componenent to cheerleading
          choreography.

> Recognize this? Humble beginnings that would turn into gold.

Missy, Torrance and Darcy clutch their knees off to one side.

                    MISSY
          I gotta parle it.

                    TORRANCE
          Don't parle it.

          JAN
     Uck with an 'F'... me.

TORRANCE spies on them from the crowd. Missy joins. Torrance
chews a hangnail. Missy tugs Tor away.

          MISSY
     Come on, don't watch this. Let's hit the
     chambre de poudre.

Missy literally yanks Torrance away from the performance as
they head to

ANOTHER PART OF CSDH CAMPUS - CONTINUOUS

the restrooms. Missy is mimicking Clover moves, trying to
get Tor to laugh. Torrance giggles, then freezes. Shock,
then horror, then tears-a-welling.

          TORRANCE
        (quietly, heart breaking)
     Buzz?

Missy reacts to

BUZZ AND A GIRL

leaning against the Tracker in face-sucking passion. RED
RINGLETS blow in the wind. Hey, BIG RED, you big slut!
They're flirting, kissing and moving towards the
dorm...unaware they are being watched.

MISSY shepherds Torrance away, toward the restroom.

          MISSY
     Okay, you didn't see that. Ohmigod ohmigod,
     okay come on, come on --

BACK AT THE COMPETITION

Another SQUAD in BROWN & GOLD carries MINITRAMPS and BANNERS,
the equipment looks exactly like the FDS equipment. Kasey
looks at Jan, concerned.

          JAN
     Coinkydink. Always the same props, it's how
     you use them that counts. It's Rancho
     Cucamonga. They don't have the stunts, or
     the tumbling, or... do they even have a
     school?

IN THE RESTROOM

Hat on a hat
confession!
Big Red and
Buzz were an
item in first
draft.

6/9/99   89.

154 EXT. INDIANA JONES THEATER - NIGHT   154

     ENTRYWAY PLACARDS read: FINALS

155 INT. BACKSTAGE AREA   155

     An ESPN INTERVIEWER readies his crew for an interview with
     Coach Shelton.

     In the b.g., Courtney, Darcy, Whitney and Jan watch the
     spectacle with disbelief.

                         ESPN INTERVIEWER
               We're talking to Anita Shelton,
               coach of the five-time national
               championship Titans from San
               Diego, California. Your thoughts
               on the competition?

                         COACH SHELTON
               It involves a great deal of hard
               work. We really need more
               competitions like it - it's for
               such a great cause.

                         ESPN INTERVIEWER
               What cause?

                         COACH SHELTON
                    (Save the Children tone)
               Advancing the sport of
               cheerleading! I just hope I live
               to see the day, when
               cheerleaders...have cheerleaders.

Just when you thought she was dead, I had to try to keep that line in for one last gasp. Sigh.

156 INT. INDIANA JONES THEATER   156

     TV CAMERAS and VARIOUS CREW ready the venue. GRIPS and SOUND
     PEOPLE hustle about.

157 INT. JUDGES PANEL   157

     At the dais behind the bleachers, TEN JUDGES ready their
     scorecards.

158 INT. BACKSTAGE AREA   158

     Isis - for the first time - looks petrified. Various Clovers
     stretch, pray and pray some more.

     VARIOUS COMPETITORS grab their stomachs and run off to puke.

122   EXT. UCLA STADIUM - DAY   122

A huge BRUINS FOOTBALL game is in progress. MARCHING BAND,
FANS, BROUHAHAH and --

the UCLA BRUINS CHEERLEADING SQUAD dominating the sidelines
in a blaze of movement. A familiar figure hits her lift and
smiles. It's none other than ISIS.

The camera pans, revealing squad-mate Torrance -- smiling,
yelling and cheering with a vengeance for those national
television cameras.

As we zoom into Torrance's mug, her familiar Orange County
inflection bursts through in VOICE-OVER.

                    TORRANCE (V.O.)
          Dear International Olympic Committee, I'm
          writing hoping you'll consider a new sport
          for the exhibition spot at the next
          Olympics...

Torrance winks at the camera as we go to black and roll

CREDITS:

Out-takes -- exaggerated Jackie Chan-esque falls, fuck-ups,
bleepers, bloops and blunders of cheerleading fiascoes. FAKE
BLOOD, FAKE DISMEMBERED LIMBS and STAGED PRATFALLS are mixed
with the real thing. Like...Justin - in cheerleading garb -
doing a standing back flip, then lifting his partner, smiling
hormonally, glancing up at the butt he is clutching. More
blood and guts until you get to the final credit and...

123   A B-BALL COURT

Torrance cheers alone on a basketball court.

                    TORRANCE
          You're history, buh-bye, like get-a-life and
          fly, I mean it's over, it's done and
          cheer-lead-ing is number - --

                                        CUTS TO BLACK:

                    TORRANCE (V.O.)
          Hey! Yo! Mr.Cinematog-whatever, Mr. Editor,
          I'm still here! (beat) Fine. You're
          jealous, middle-aged men who can't deal with
          my power. Be that way. Audience! You
          viewers! If you wanna see my butt, yell,
          'butt'!

Handwritten margin notes:

UCLA BRUINS - tried to put a bow on everything and that wasn't needed - so extra! Told you I had six endings.

I love that this happened and cheer was almost a provisional sport or an exhibition sport at the Olympics in 2020.

I thought a fake blooper reel with injuries would have been hilarious. It's tonally too much and that's the thing about going a bit too far - you can always pull it back...

This is super camp and that campy tone - of drag queens and gay men - was definitely something I was experimenting with.

I do enjoy the shout-out re: patriarchy 20+ years before that was having a moment.

6/13/97   p.116

> I think we can all agree - she ready for a 40-page haircut.

After a beat, Torrance flashes back on the screen, back to camera, skirt up, spankies in full bloom. After standing a beat, she turns around, surprised, not realizing she was back on.

                TORRANCE
Eww. You are so perverted! I love that about you. Come on back now, ya hear? I'm nothing without you, and it's super important that we stay in --

> This was meant to be a-dorkable and very "I'm just a girl" Gwen Stefani-esque. Not sure breaking the 4th wall was helping anyone.

It cuts to black before she can finish.

                TORRANCE (V.O.)
Hey!

                            THE END

PART THREE:
THE ALL YOU PART

CHAPTER TWELVE

The All You Part

INT. YOUR MIND

YOU are finishing this book experiment. We're in your head
now.

>   YOU
> Maybe this is easy for you to say,
> but you're driving me a bit nuts
> and I don't even know what to write
> yet. I really don't know what I'm
> doing. I don't even know if I
> understand these suggestions. Or if
> I can tell stories --

>   ME
> We all start somewhere. This isn't
> about me. Or knowing the answers.
> It's about trying. And learning.
> Know-it-alls are boring. Curious
> folks change the world. Be curious!

>   YOU
> I don't know what I want.

>   ME
> Secret Truth of Adulting?
>   (sweet whisper)
> No one knows anything.

>   YOU
> What if I suck?

>   ME
> Oh, you will. I promise. You
> absolutely will suck. Just accept
> it. Don't fight it. Embrace it. We
> all suck at times. There's no
> getting around it.

>   YOU
> I'm really freaked out. I really
> don't know if I can do this.

>   ME
> It's about freaking out and trying
> anyway. Just try. And keep trying.
> You may fall. You get up. You fall.
>   (MORE)

                         ME (CONT'D)
         If you don't like the process, find
         a different process. There are many
         places to plant your creativity.

                         YOU
         What if I hate it? What if people
         make fun of me? I'm still scared.

                         ME
         We all get scared. It's normal.
         Breathing and meditation put the
         central nervous system in a very
         nice state for creativity. Lots has
         been written about this.

                         YOU
         Meditation won't help me if I get
         cancelled!

                         ME
         Consider embracing 'learning
         culture' instead of 'win-lose'
         culture. If the Toros had been
         cancelled, there'd be no story.
         Torrance is humiliated 'just
         enough' to learn, but not so much
         she freezes from the trauma and
         can't recover. We have to stop
         shaming teachable moments in ways
         where lessons get totally lost.

                         YOU
         I will meditate. I will consider
         being someone who looks for win-
         wins. You can go now, please.

                         ME
         Remember: besides imagining a
         story, remember to imagine best
         version of people. Especially if
         they cannot yet see it. Especially
         if that person is you.

And like that? Let's ROLL CREDITS.

FOR YOUR CONSIDERATION

Screenplays are an esoteric form and it's like the Wild West out there... but here are some suggestions on how you can tap into resources. Go to my website for promo codes.

1) Consider some screenwriting software. There are many brands from low cost to no cost. I use Final Draft.

2) Consider professional feedback. I recommend the Blacklist for evaluations of your script. The Blacklist is a top industry screenplay site that holds contests and also provides evaluations on scripts. Some huge movies have been featured on The Blacklist before they were made -- Juno, In Bruges, and The Social Network, to name a few! You will pay for the evaluation, but you can see how you stack up.

3) Consider taking a class. UCB, Groundlings, Second City, or any number of classes nationwide. UCB has sketch-writing classes. The idea is simple: hive-mind can give you a fun creative buzz. Connecting with like-minded people helps you buddy up and keep each other accountable.

4) Consider entering your work into screenwriting labs or competitions. This will give you a deadline to meet and a concrete goal to work towards. I did not get into the Sundance Screenwriting Lab but ended up mentoring for them in Park City and in Brazil.

● ● ●

"I don't think anything will change in Hollywood until we have more than 1% of women directors on the top grossing films. As long as those statistics remain the same, it's very much like Saudi Arabia or the Catholic Church. If you have a society that systematically excludes the hearts and brains of women, you're going to have a sick, warped society."
MAUREEN DOWD

"Because our culture was built upon and benefits from the control of women. The way power justifies controlling a group is by conditioning thee masses to believe that the group cannot be trusted. So the campaign to convince us to mistrust women begins early...and comes from everywhere."
GLENNON DOYLE,
UNTAMED

"Perfectionism is a particularly evil lure for women, who, I believe, hold themselves to an even higher standard of performance than do men. There are many reasons why women's voices and visions are not more widely represented today in creative fields. Some of that exclusion is due to regular old misogyny, but it's also true that—all too often—women are the ones holding themselves back from participating in the first place....We must understand that the drive for perfectionism is a corrosive waste of time, because nothing is ever beyond criticism. No matter how many hours you spend attempting to render something flawless, somebody will always be able to find fault with it. (There are people out there who still consider Beethoven's symphonies a little bit too, you know, loud.) At some point, you really just have to finish your work and release it as is—if only so that you can go on to make other things with a glad and determined heart. Which is the entire point. Or should be."
ELIZABETH GILBERT,
BIG MAGIC: CREATIVE LIVING BEYOND FEAR

"We've noticed a pattern....we don't see this when we have men on. The comments are super mean and critical. Always before they've listened. There's been a lot of quick judgment when we have strong female guests on, who are known to have opinions. Versus men....A pretty clear pattern. Your feed can be as negative as you want it to be. We try to keep it positive. Positivity is contagious. Negativity is the same way."

MONICA PADMAN,
CO-HOST ARMCHAIR EXPERT
EPISODE 92: "CHELSEA HANDLER"
APRIL 1, 2019

"I don't care about adulation from people I don't know. So celebrity is this huge, gaping — fame is a huge disappointment. For those of you who are listening who want to be famous, just do something else. It's not what you think it is. It's toxic."

SIA FURLER,
THE TIM FERRISS SHOW
EPISODE 452
AUGUST 13, 2020

RESOURCES

ABC WRITERS' PROGRAM
www.abctalentdevelopment.com/writing_program.html

AUSTIN FILM FESTIVAL
www.austinfilmfestival.com/submit

FINAL DRAFT BIG BREAK COMPETITION
www.finaldraft.com/big-break-screenwriting-contest

GROUNDLINGS
www.groundlings.com

HBO ACCESS WRITING FELLOWSHIP
www.hbo.com/hboaccess/writing

KAIROS PRIZE
www.kairosprize.com

NBC WRITERS-ON-THE-VERGE
www.nbcunitips.com/category/programs/writers

OUTFEST SCREENWRITER'S LAB (LGBTQ+)
www.outfest.org/submissions

PAGE INTERNATIONAL SCREENWRITING AWARDS
www.pageawards.com/the-contest

SCREENCRAFT SCREENWRITING FELLOWSHIP
www.screencraft.org/fellowship

SCRIPTD
www.scriptd.com

SECOND CITY
www.secondcity.com

SLAMDANCE
www.slamdance.com/screenplay

STAFF ME UP
www.stafmeup.com

SUNDANCE SCREENWRITERS AND EPISODIC LABS
apply.sundance.org

THE BLACKLIST
www.blcklst.com

THE NICHOLL FELLOWSHIPS
www.oscars.org/nicholl/about

UCB
www.ucbcomedy.com

WB TELEVISION WRITERS' WORKSHOP
televisionworkshop.warnerbros.com

WRITER'S GUILD OF AMERICA
www.wga.org

BE YOUR OWN SUPERHERO

+ RESCUE YOUR IDEAS
BECAUSE THEY MATTER

What you care about matters.

It's ok to care about what you care about.

Don't apologize for it.

Respect it.

Respect what you care about.

Just love it.

Love what you care about.

Start there.

Write about it.

Intrigue and delight in it.

Focus on what you care about.

Dare to dance with it.

Place a benevolent gaze upon what you care about.

Don't worry about what other people think.

This is what the world needs more of.

People sharing what they care about.

People respecting what they care about.

Respecting it enough to focus love and patience and attention upon it.

Placing that energy and care upon what matters.

Upon what matters to you.

Lift it out of distress.

Lift it out of the gutter of your judgement.

Lift it up and away from any need for certainty.

Protect it from those who would shame it. Or you.

Scoop up what matters and hold it.

If someone shames it, say: "Excuse me. Have a nice day." And give that shame no oxygen.

Give it no space in your precious head.

Direct your eyes towards the prize of what matters.

Lift it up in your arms and treasure it and relish this: you are someone who cares.

Support your efforts with the kindness of a good parent.

Be patient with it and yourself in ways that feel good.

Respect these efforts in those who are trying to do the same.

Cultivate this capacity in yourself.

Encourage this light in others.

Love what you love.

Love others who love.

Love well and freely and bravely.

Love the love itself.

Uplift and elevate and magnify the things you care about.

Rescue your ideas because they matter.

Be a hero for what you care about.

Believe you are the person you can look up to.

Do this, and your authentic voice will shine through.

That's point of view.

That's being a hero for what you care about.

Be your own superhero.

The world needs you.

This book is dedicated to my mom.

SPECIAL THANKS:
Gail Fanaro, Shauna Driscoll, Warren Etheredge + The Writer's Guild of America

If you would like to purchase a license to perform CHEER FEVER
- the original screenplay for BRING IT ON -
live in front of an audience,
PLEASE EMAIL: VERVEBALL@GMAIL.COM
OR
WWW.JESSICABENDINGER.COM
to legally license to the original dramatic stage rights.
Thank you.

CPSIA information can be obtained
at www.ICGtesting.com
Printed in the USA
BVHW011428121220
595578BV00017B/716